E.

M. Spratt de

FLORA AND THALIA;

OR,

GEMS OF FLOWERS AND POETRY.

YE ARE THE STARS OF EARTH,—AND DEAR TO ME
IS EACH SMALL TWINKLING GEM THAT WANDERS FREE
'MID GLADE OR WOODLAND, OR BY MURM'RING STREAM,
FOR YE TO ME ARE MORE THAN SWEET OR FAIR,
I LOVE YE FOR THE MEM'RIES THAT YE BEAR
OF BY-GONE HOURS, WHOSE BLISS WAS BUT A DREAM.

LOUISA ANNE TWAMLEY.

Flora and Thalia: Or, Gems of Flowers and Poetry, by a Lady

Flora

M. Spratt. del.

FLORA AND THALIA;

OR

Gems of Flowers and Poetry;

BEING AN ALPHABETICAL ARRANGEMENT OF FLOWERS, WITH
APPROPRIATE POETICAL ILLUSTRATIONS,

EMBELLISHED WITH COLOURED PLATES.

BY A LADY.

" Not a Tree,
A Plant, a Leaf, a Blossom, but contains
A folio volume."

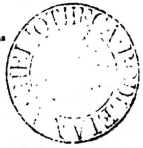

LONDON:
PRINTED FOR HENRY WASHBOURNE,
SALISBURY SQUARE.

———

M DCCC XXXV.

137.

600002300B

35.

137.

FLORA AND THALIA;

OR,

GEMS OF FLOWERS AND POETRY.

E.

M.Sp.

M. Spratt. del.

forth those ideas which all should possess when they contemplate nature, " always pleasing, everywhere lovely."

The care and attention bestowed on the moral and poetical department, will, she hopes, insure, at least, a small share of approbation.

The coloured plates which illustrate the poetry, were taken from nature ; and are as botanically correct as so small a work will admit.   The descriptive part is from Woodville, Sir James Smith, Rousseau, the Hortus Canta-brigiensis, and other scientific works of later date.

King's Road, Chelsea.

CONTENTS.

INTRODUCTORY POEMS.

SEASONS, FLOWERS, ETC.

FLORA ALPHABETICA.

WITH POETICAL ILLUSTRATIONS.

MISCELLANEOUS POEMS.

DIRECTIONS FOR PLACING THE PLATES.

The WREATH, a presentation Plate, to *follow the half-title.*

The EVENING PRIMROSE, *Plate E,* to front the title *as a fron-tispiece.*

The twenty-four Flowers to face their *botanical descriptions.*

FLORA AND THALIA;

OR,

GEMS OF FLOWERS AND POETRY.

———

AN ODE TO SPRING.

Now the golden morn aloft
　Waves her dew-bespangled wing,
With vermeil cheek, and whisper soft,
　She wooes the tardy spring;
Till April starts, and calls around
The sleeping fragrance from the ground;
And lightly, o'er the living scene,
Scatters his freshest tend'rest green.

New-born flocks, in rustic dance,
　Frisking ply their feeble feet;
Forgetful of their wintry trance,
　The birds his presence greet.

B

But chief the skylark warbles high
His trembling thrilling ecstasy,
And lessening from the dazzled sight,
Melts into air and liquid light.

Rise my soul! on wings of fire,
   Rise the rapt'reus choir among;
Hark! 'tis Nature strikes the lyre,
   And leads the general song.
Warm let the lyric transport flow,
Warm as the ray that bids it glow,
And animates the vernal grove
With health, with harmony, and love.

Yesterday, the sullen year
   Saw the snowy whirlwind fly;
Mute was the music of the air,
   The herd stood drooping by;
Their raptures now that wildly flow,
No yesterday, nor morrow, know;
'Tis man alone that joy descries,
With forward and reverted eyes.

See the wretch, that long has tost
   On the thorny bed of pain,
At length repair his vigour lost,
   And breathe, and walk again.
The meanest floweret of the vale,
The simplest note that swells the gale,
The common sun, the air, the skies,
To him are opening paradise.

                   GRAY.

APRIL.

Now infant April joins the Spring,
  And views the wat'ry sky;
As youngling linnet tries its wing,
  And fears at first to fly.
With timid step she ventures on,
  And hardly dares to smile;
Till blossoms open one by one,
  And sunny hours beguile.

In wanton gambols, like a child,
  She tends her early toils;
And seeks the buds along the wild,
  That blossom while she smiles:
Or, laughing on, with nought to chide,
  She races with the hours;
Or sports by Nature's lovely side,
  And fills her lap with flow'rs.

The shepherd, on his pasture-walks,
  The first fair cowslip finds,
Whose tufted flowers, on slender stalks,
  Keep nodding to the winds.
And though the thorns withhold the May,
  Their shades the violets bring,
Which children stoop for in their play,
  As tokens of the Spring.

B 2

Sweet month! thy pleasures bid thee be
 The fairest child of Spring;
And every hour that comes with thee,
 Comes some new joy to bring:
The trees still deeper in their bloom,
 Grass greens the meadow lands;
And flowers with ev'ry morning come,
 As dropt by fairy hands.

The field and garden's lovely hours
 Begin and end with thee;
For what's so sweet as peeping flowers,
 And bursting buds to see?
What time the dew's unsullied drops,
 In burnish'd gold distil,
On crocus flowers' unclosing tops,
 And drooping daffodil?

To see thee come, all hearts rejoice,
 And warm with feelings strong;
With thee all Nature finds a voice,
 And hums a waking song.
The lover views thy welcome hours,
 And thinks of summer come;
And takes the maid thy early flowers,
 To tempt her steps from home.

Though, at her birth, the northern gale
 Come with its withering sigh;
And hopeful blossoms, turning pale,
 Upon her bosom die;

Ere April seeks another place,
　And ends her reign in this,
She leaves us with as fair a face,
　As e'er gave birth to bliss.

CLARE.

THE GREENHOUSE.

WHO loves a garden, loves a greenhouse too;
Unconscious of a less propitious clime,
There blooms exotic beauty, warm and snug,
While the winds whistle, and the snows descend;
The spiry myrtle, with unwithering leaf,
Shines there, and flourishes.　The golden boast
Of Portugal, and western India, there
The ruddier orange, and the paler lime,
Peep through their polished foliage at the storm,
And seem to smile at what they need not fear.
The amomum there, with intermingling flow'rs
And cherries, hangs her twigs.　Geranium boasts
Her crimson honours; and the spangled beau
Ficoides glitters bright the winter long.
All plants, of every leaf, that can endure
The winter's frown, if screen'd from his shrewd bite,
Live there and prosper;—those Ausonia claims,
Levantine regions these; th' Azores send
Their jessamine, her jessamine, remote
Caffraria; foreigners from many lands,
They form one social shade, as if conven'd

B 3

By magic summons of th' Orpheian lyre;
Yet just arrangement, rarely brought to pass
But by a master's hand, disposing well
The gay diversities of leaf and flow'r,
Must lend its aid t' illustrate all their charms,
And dress the regular, yet various scene.
Plant behind plant aspiring, in the van
The dwarfish; in the rear retir'd, but still
Sublime above the rest, the statelier stand.
So once were ranged the sons of ancient Rome,
A noble show! while Roscius trod the stage;
And so, while Garrick, as renowned as he,
The sons of Albion; fearing each to lose
Some note of Nature's music from his lips,
And covetous of Shakspeare's beauty, seen
In every flash of his far-beaming eye.
Nor taste alone, and well-contriv'd display
Suffice to give the marshall'd ranks the grace
Of their complete effect.   Much yet remains
Unsung, and many cares are yet behind,.
And more laborious; cares on which depends
Their vigour, injur'd soon, not soon restor'd.
The soil must be renew'd, which, often wash'd,
Loses its treasure of salubrious salts,
And disappoints the roots; the slender roots
Close interwoven, where they meet the vase
Must smooth be shorn away; the sapless branch
Must fly before the knife; the wither'd leaf
Must be detach'd, and where it strews the floor,
Swept with a woman's neatness, breeding else
Contagion, and disseminating death.

Discharge but these kind offices, (and who
Would spare, that loves them, offices like these?)
Well they reward the toil.   The sight is pleas'd;
The scent regal'd ; each odorif'rous leaf,
Each op'ning blossom, freely breathes abroad
Its gratitude, and thanks him with its sweets.

COWPER.

GARDENING.

———— To deck the shapely knoll,
That softly swell'd, and gaily dress'd, appears
A flow'ry island from the dark green lawn
Emerging, must be deem'd a labour due
To no mean hand, and asks the touch of taste.
Here also grateful mixture of well-match'd
And sorted hues, (each giving each relief,
And by contrasted beauty shining more,)
Is needful.   Strength may wield the pond'rous spade,
May turn the clod, and wheel the compost home ;
But elegance, chief grace the garden shows,
And most attractive, is the fair result
Of thought, the creature of a polish'd mind.
Without it, all is gothic as the scene
To which th' insipid citizen resorts
Near yonder heath ; where industry misspent,
But proud of his uncouth ill-chosen task,
Has made a heaven on earth ; with suns and moons

Of covert close, where scarce a speck of day
Falls on the lengthen'd gloom, protracted sweeps—
Now meets the bending sky; the river now
Dimpling along, the breezy ruffled lake,
The forest dark'ning round, the glitt'ring spire,
Th' ethereal mountain, and the distant main.
But why so far extensive? when, at hand,
Along these blushing borders, bright with dew,
And, in yon mingled wilderness of flow'rs,
Fair-handed Spring unbosoms ev'ry grace;
Throws out the snow-drop and the crocus first;
The daisy, primrose, violet darkly blue,
And polyanthus of unnumber'd dyes;
The yellow wall-flower, stained with iron brown;
And lavish stock, that scents the garden round:
From the soft wing of vernal breezes shed,   ·
Anemones; auriculas, enrich'd
With shining meal o'er all their velvet leaves;
And full ranunculus, of glowing red.
Then comes the tulip-race, where beauty plays
Her idle freaks: from family diffused
To family, as flies the father-dust,
The varied colours run; and while they break
On the charm'd eye, th' exulting florist marks,
With secret pride, the wonders of his hand.
No gradual bloom is wanting; from the bud,
First boon of Spring, to Summer's musky tribes:
Nor hyacinths, of purest virgin white,
Low-bent, and blushing inward; nor jonquils
Of potent fragrance; nor narcissus fair,
As o'er the fabled fountain hanging still;

Nor broad carnations, nor gay-spotted pinks;
Nor, shower'd from ev'ry bush, the damask rose.
Infinite numbers, delicacies, smells,
With hues on hues expression cannot paint,
The breath of Nature, and her endless bloom.

THOMSON.

THE CHAPLET.

To thee, sweet Maid, I bring,
The beauteous progeny of Spring:
In every breathing bloom I find
Some pleasing emblem of thy mind.
The blushes of that op'ning rose,
Thy tender modesty disclose;
These snow-white lilies of the vale,
Diffusing fragrance to the gale,
No ostentatious tints assume,
Vain of their exquisite perfume;
Careless, and sweet, and mild, we see
In these a lovely type of thee.
On yonder gay enamell'd green,
That azure blossom smil'd serene;
Not changing with the changeful sky,
Its faithless tints inconstant fly;
For, unimpair'd by winds and rain,
I saw th' unalter'd hue remain:

So were thy mild affections prov'd,
Thy heart, by fortune's frown unmov'd,
Pleas'd to administer relief,
Would solace and alleviate grief.
These flowers with genuine beauty glow;
The tints from Nature's pencil flow.
What artist could improve their bloom,
Or 'meliorate their sweet perfume?
Fruitless the vain attempt!   Like these,
Thy native truth,—thine artless ease,
Fair, unaffected maid, can never fail to please.

RICHARDSON.

THE CLOSE OF SPRING.

THE garlands fade that Spring so lately wove,
   Each simple flower which she has nursed in dew, —
Anemones, that spangled every grove;
   The Primrose wan, and Harebell mildly blue :
No more shall Violets linger in the dell,
   Or purple Orchis variegate the plain :
Till Spring again shall call forth every bell,
   And dress with humid hands her wreaths again.
Oh poor humanity ! so frail, so fair,
   Are the fond visions of thy early day ;
Till tyrant passion, and corrosive care,
   Bid all thy fairy colours fade away !
Another May new buds and flowers shall bring :
   Ah ! why has happiness no second Spring?

CHARLES SMITH.

MAY.

Born in yon blaze of orient sky,
　Sweet May! thy radiant form unfold;
Unclose thy blue and tender eye,
　And wave thy shadowy locks of gold.

For thee the fragrant zephyrs blow,
　For thee descends the sunny shower;
The rills in softer murmur flow,
　And brighter blossoms gem the bower.

DARWIN.

THE SUMMER'S CALL.

Come away! the sunny hours
Woo thee far to founts and bowers!
O'er the very waters now,
　　　　In their play,
Flowers are shedding beauty's glow,
　　　　Come away!
Where the lily's tender gleam
Quivers on the glowing stream,
　　　　Come away !

c

All the air is filled with sound,
Soft, and sultry, and profound ;
Murmurs through the shadowy grass
                    Lightly stray ;
Faint winds whisper, as they pass,
                    Come away !
Where the bee's deep music swells,
From the trembling fox-glove bells—
                    Come away !

In the deep heart of the rose,
Now the crimson love-hue glows ;
Now the glow-worm's lamp, by night,
                    Sheds a ray,
Dreary, starry, greenly bright,—
                    Come away !
Where the fairy cup-moss lies,
With the wild wood-strawberries,
                    Come away !

                              MRS. HEMANS.

SUMMER—THE TROPICS.

BEAR me, Pomona, to thy citron groves ;
To where the lemon, and the piercing lime,
With the deep orange, glowing through the green,
Their lighter glories blend.   Lay me reclined
Beneath the spreading tamarind that shakes,
Fanned by the breeze, its ever-cooling fruit.
Deep in the night the massy locust sheds,
Quench my hot limbs ; or lead me through the maze,
Embowering endless, of the Indian fig :
Or thrown at gayer ease, on some fair brow,
Let me behold, by breezy murmurs cooled,
Broad o'er my head the verdant cedars wave,
And high palmettos lift their graceful shade.
Or stretched amid these orchards of the sun,
Give me to drain the cocoa's milky bowl,
And from the palm to draw its freshening wine,
More bounteous far than all the frantic juice
Which Bacchus pours.   Nor, on its slender twigs,
Low bending, be the full pomegranate scorned ;
Nor, creeping through the wood, the gelid race
Of berries.   Oft in humble station dwells
Unboastful worth, above fastidious pomp.
Witness, thou best Anana ! thou, the pride
Of vegetable life, beyond whate'er
The poets fabled in the golden age :
Quick let me strip thee of thy tufty coat,   ·
Spread thy ambrosial store, and feast with Jove.

THOMSON.

c 2

SUMMER MORNING.

AWAKE! the morning shines, and the fresh fields
Call you : ye lose the prime to mark how spring
The tender plants ; how blows the citron grove ;
What drops the myrrh, and what the balmy reed ;
How Nature paints her colours ; how the bee
Sits on the bloom extracting liquid sweets.

MILTON.

INVITATION TO SOLITUDE.

———— BUT when the sun
Shakes from his noon-day throne the scatt'ring clouds,
E'en shooting listless languor through the deeps ;
Then seek the bank where flow'ring elders crowd ;
Where, scatter'd wild, the lily of the vale
Its balmy essence breathes ; where cowslips hang
The dewy head ; where purple violets lurk
With all the lowly children of the shade ;
Or lie reclin'd beneath yon spreading ash
Hung o'er the steep, whence, borne on liquid wing,
The sounding culver shoots ; or where the hawk
High in the beetling cliff his aerie builds.
There let the classic page thy fancy lead
Through rural scenes, such as the Mantuan swain
Paints in the matchless harmony of song ;

Or catch thyself the landscape, gliding swift
Athwart imagination's vivid eye:
Or by the vocal woods and waters lull'd,
And lost in lonely musing, in the dream,
Confus'd, of careless solitude, where mix
Ten thousand wand'ring images of things,
Soothe ev'ry gust of passion into peace;
All but the swellings of the soften'd heart,
That waken, not disturb, the tranquil mind.

THOMSON.

THE PARTING OF SUMMER.

Thou'rt bearing hence the roses,
  Glad Summer, fare thee well!
Thou'rt singing thy last melodies
  In every wood and dell.

Brightly, sweet Summer! brightly
  Thine hours have floated by,
To the joyous birds of the woodland boughs,
  The rangers of the sky.

And brightly in the forest,
  To the wild deer wandering free;
And brightly, 'midst the garden flowers,
  To the happy murmuring bee.

c 3

But, oh! thou gentle Summer,
　　If I greet thy flowers once more,
Bring me again the buoyancy
　　Wherewith my soul should soar!

MRS. HEMANS.

AUTUMN.

WHEN the bright Virgin gives the beauteous days,
And Libra weighs in equal scales the year;
From heaven's high cope, with fierce effulgence shook,
Of parting Summer, a serener blue,
With golden light enlivened, wide invests
The happy world. Attempered suns arise,
Sweet-beamed, and shedding oft through lucid clouds
A pleasing calm; while broad and brown below,
Extensive harvests hang the heavy head.
Rich, silent, deep, they stand; for not a gale
Rolls its light billows o'er the bending plain:
A calm of plenty! till the ruffled air
Falls from its poise, and gives the breeze to blow.
Rent is the fleecy mantle of the sky;
The clouds fly different; and the sudden sun
By fits effulgent gilds the illumined fields,
And black by fits the shadows sweep along.
A gaily-chequered, heart-expanding view,
Far as the circling eye can shoot around,
Unbounded tossing in a flood of corn.

THOMSON.

L'AUTOMNE.

SALUT, bois couronnés d'un reste de verdure !
  Feuillages jaunissans sur les gazons épars !
Salut, derniers beaux jours ! le deuil de la nature
  Convient à ma douleur, et plait à mes regards.

Oui, dans ces jours d'Automne où la nature expire,
  A ses regards voilés je trouve plus d'attraits.
C'est l'adieu d'un ami, c'est le dernier sourire
  Des lèvres que la mort va fermer pour jamais.

Ainsi, prêt à quitter l'horizon de la vie,
  Pleurant de mes longs jours l'espoir évanoui,
Je me retourne encore, et d'un regard d'envie
  Je contemple ses biens dont je n'ai pas joui.

Terre, soleil, vallons, belle et douce nature !
  Je vous dois une larme au bord de mon tombeau ;
L'air est si parfumé ! la lumière est si pure !
  Aux regards d'un mourant le soleil est si beau.

Je voudrais maintenant vuider jusqu' à la lie,
  Ce calice mêlé de nectar et de fiel :
Au fond de cette coupe où je buvais la vie,
  Peutêtre restait-il une goutte de miel !

La fleur tombe en livrant ses parfums au zéphire,
  A la vie, au soleil, ce sont là ses adieux ;
Moi, je meurs : et mon âme, au moment qu'elle expire,
  S'exhale comme un son triste et mélodieux.

                                   DE LAMARTINE.

WINTER.

'Tis done ! dread Winter spreads its latest glooms,
And reigns tremendous o'er the conquered year.
How dead the vegetable kingdom lies !
How dumb the tuneful ! Horror wide extends
His desolate domain.   Behold, fond man !
See here thy pictured life ; pass some few years,
Thy flowering Spring, thy Summer's ardent strength,
Thy sober Autumn fading into age ;
And pale concluding Winter comes at last,
And shuts the scene.

                                   THOMSON.

DECEMBER.

No mark of vegetable life is seen ;
  No bird to bird repeats his tuneful call,
Save the dark leaves of some rude evergreen ;
  Save the lone redbreast on the moss-grown wall.

                                   SCOTT.

THE SEASONS.

WHEN snows descend, and robe the fields
   In winter's bright array :
Touched by the sun the lustre fades,
   And weeps itself away.

When Spring appears ; when violets blow,
   And shed a rich perfume ;
How soon the fragrance breathes its last,
   How short-liv'd is its bloom.

Fresh in the morn, the summer rose
   Hangs withering ere 'tis noon ;
We scarce enjoy the balmy gift,
   But mourn the pleasure gone.

With gliding fire, an evening star
   Streaks the autumnal skies ;
Shook from the sphere, it darts away,
   And in an instant dies.

Such are the charms that flush the cheek,
   And sparkle in the eye ;
So from the lovely finish'd form,
   The transient graces fly.

To this the seasons as they roll,
  Their attestation bring ;
They warn the fair ; their every round
  Confirm the truth I sing.

HERVEY.

CHOICE OF SEASONS.

Who loves not Spring's voluptuous hours,
The carnival of birds and flowers?
Yet who would choose, however dear,
That Spring should revel all the year?
Who loves not Summer's splendid reign,
The bridal of the earth and main?
Yet who would choose, however bright,
A dog-day noon without a night?
Who loves not Autumn's joyous round,
When corn, and wine, and oil abound?
Yet who would choose, however gay,
A year of unrenewed decay?
Who loves not Winter's awful form?
The sphere-born music of the storm?
Yet who would choose, how grand soever,
The shortest day to last for ever?

MONTGOMERY.

——————— WHO CAN PAINT
LIKE NATURE? CAN IMAGINATION BOAST,
AMID ITS GAY CREATION, HUES LIKE HERS?
OR CAN IT MIX THEM WITH THAT MATCHLESS SKILL,
AND LOSE THEM IN EACH OTHER, AS APPEARS
IN EV'RY BUD THAT BLOWS? IF FANCY THEN,
UNEQUAL, FAILS BENEATH THE PLEASING TASK,
AH! WHAT SHALL LANGUAGE DO? AH, WHERE FIND WORDS
TING'D WITH SO MANY COLOURS?

THOMSON.

A.

ANEMONE PRATENSIS.

(Meadow Anemone.)

THIS Anemone is perennial, and a native of Germany, where it grows in open fields, flowering in May. It was first cultivated by Mr. Millar, in the year 1731; and as we now find it in our gardens, it very much resembles the Anemone Pulsatilla. The principal distinctions between these species, as they grow naturally, are taken from the flower, which in the Anemone Pratensis is more pendulous, smaller, of a darker colour, and has the apices of the petals reflexed; the stem, also, is less hairy and shorter than that of the Pulsatilla. The Anemone, or Pasque flower, so called from its flowering about Easter, adorns some of our dry chalky hills with its beautiful purple flowers. . The garden Anemones, which are so ornamental to the flower borders in the spring, are only of two species, notwithstanding the variety of their colours. Art, to increase their beauty, has rendered them very large and double.

Baron Stoerck has recommended this plant as an effectual remedy for most diseases affecting the eye;

D

and many German physicians have since tried its effects, and with success. Every part of this plant was recommended by Baron Stoerck for medicinal purposes. The flowers have scarcely any smell.

Class, POLYANDRIA.　*Order*, POLYGYNIA.

THE ANEMONE.

SEE yon Anemones their leaves unfold,
With rubies flaming, and with living gold;
In silken robes each hillock stands arrayed.
Be gay! too soon the flowers of Spring will fade:
Ah! crop the flowers of pleasure while they blow,
Ere Winter hides them in a veil of snow.
Youth, like a thin Anemone, displays
His silken leaf, and in a morn decays.

SIR WM. JONES, *from the Persian.*

THE ANEMONE.

SHORT time ensued, till where the blood * was shed,
A flower began to raise its purple head;
Still here the fate of lovely forms we see,
So sudden fades the sweet Anemone:
The feeble stems to stormy blasts a prey,
Their sickly beauties droop and pine away;
Their winds forbid the flowers to flourish long,
Which owe to winds their name in Grecian song †.

EUSDEN, *from Ovid.*

FROM the soft wing of vernal breezes shed,
Anemones; auriculas enriched
With shining meal o'er all their velvet leaves;
And full ranunculus, of glowing red.

THOMSON.

* The ancient writers inform us, that Venus, in her grief
for the loss of Adonis, mingled her tears with his blood; from
whence sprang an Anemone, the first ever seen.

† Anemone is derived from the Greek ανημος, the wind;
and hence is called the wind-flower.

D 2

BLUE, OR HAREBELL.

(*Non scriptus.*)

THIS beautiful little flower is a native of Persia; but is found in most parts of Europe. Our woods in the Spring present a lively appearance, from the mixture of their azure blue bells among the pale yellow primroses, and the many different tinted heaths, so tastefully intermingled by the hand of Nature. It is called Harebell from its generally growing in those places frequented by hares: the flower varies in colour and beauty; some being completely white, and others much resembling the poorer kinds of hyacinths; but they have longer and narrower flowers, not swelling at the bottom: the bunch of flowers is likewise longer and bends downwards. The fresh roots of this plant are said to be poisonous; the juice is mucilaginous, and in the time of Queen Elizabeth was used as starch.

Class, HEXANDRIA. *Order,* MONOGYNIA.

B.

M. decrate des.

THE BLUE, OR HAREBELL.

In Spring's green lap there blooms a flower,
Whose cup imbibes each vernal shower,
That sips fresh Nature's balmy dew,
Clad in her sweetest, purest blue;
Yet shuns the ruddy eye of morning,
The shaggy wood's brown shade adorning.
Simplest floweret! Child of May!
Though hid from the broad eye of day,
Doom'd in the shade thy sweets to shed,
Unnoticed droop thy languid head:
Still Nature's darling thou'lt remain;
She feeds thee with her softest rain;
Fills each sweet bud with honied tears,
With genial gales thy bosom cheers.
Oh! then, unfold thy simple charms,
In yon deep thicket's sheltering arms.
Far from the fierce and sultry glare,
No heedless hand shall harm thee there;
Still, then, avoid the gaudy scene,
The flaunting sun, th' embroidered green,
And bloom and fade with chaste reserve, unseen.

CAROLINE SYMONDS.

BLACK HELLEBORE, or, CHRISTMAS ROSE.

(Helleborus niger.)

THE Christmas Rose, so called from its flowering about January, is perennial, and a native of Austria and Italy. It was unknown in our garden, till cultivated by Mr. John Gerard, in 1596. It has a pleasing appearance in our parterres, at a time of the year when all around it looks dull and gloomy. The Ancients used to esteem this plant a powerful remedy in maniacal diseases; but as the same effects may be produced with more certainty and safety by other medicines, the use of it is now almost entirely abandoned, as it is well known to be poisonous. However, as a great acquisition to the flower border, we recommend its cultivation.

Class, POLYANDRIA.   *Order*, POLYGYNIA.

c.

.M. Spratt del .

THE CHRISTMAS ROSE.

THE garden boasts no beauty now.
   Its summer graces all are fled;
Frost glitters on the leafless bough,
   And branch and spray alike seem dead.

Yet here, regardless of the chill,
   The sternness of the wintry hour,
One pleasing blossom greets us still,
   A fair, though unassuming flower.

In changeful life 'tis even so,
   False friends fall off when storms arise;
They shared our joy, but shun our woe,
   Like plants that fear inclement skies.

And thus the true of heart remain,
   Without one altered look or tone;
So kind we almost bless the pain,
   That makes us know such friends our own.
                    M.

THE WINTER ROSE.

HAIL, and farewell, thou lovely guest!
  I may not woo thy stay;
The hues that paint thy glowing vest,
  Are fading fast away,
Like the returning tints that die
At evening on the western sky,
And melt in misty grey.

It was but now thy radiant smile
  Broke through the season's gloom,
As bending I inhaled awhile
  Thy breathing of perfume;
And traced on every silken leaf,
A tale of summer, sweet and brief,
And sudden as thy doom.

The morning sun thy petals hail'd,
  New from their mossy cell;
At eve his beam, in sorrow veil'd,
  Bade thee a last farewell.
To-morrow's ray shall mark the spot,
Where, loosen'd from their fairy knot,
Thy withering beauties fell.

ANON.

ON THE SAME.

ALAS! on thy forsaken stem
  My heart shall long recline,
And mourn the transitory gem,
  And make the story mine!
So on my joyless winter hour
Has oped some fair and fragrant flower,
  With smile as soft as thine.

Like thee the vision came and went,
  Like thee, it bloomed and fell;
In momentary pity sent,
  Of fairy climes to tell:
So frail its form, so short its stay,
That nought the lingering heart could say,
  But hail, and fare thee well!

ANON.

DAHLIA.

(*Dahlia Georgina.*)

THIS splendid plant was originally found by Baron Humboldt, in a sandy soil in Mexico, North America. Its height varies from three to six feet. The petals of the single flower are commonly eight, but the number is variable, and in the double flowers they are exceedingly numerous. This plant was first introduced into this country in 1804, and excited so much admiration from the splendour and variety of its colours, that, we are told, florists could scarcely satisfy the demand for them. For stateliness of appearance, and richness of colouring, this flower stands unrivalled; but for fragrance it must bend even to the modest lily of the valley, or the retiring violet; although Mr. Knight says, that at one particular period of the flower's opening it has a slight, but not a fragrant smell. The varieties are very numerous, and botanists are divided as to their species. This plant received its name of Dahlia, from Cavanilles, who dedicated it to Andrew Dahl, a Swedish Botanist; and that of Georgina from Willdenow, who named it after Dr. Georgi of Petersburg. Florists differ much in the

culture and propagation of this plant, some recommending a dry situation, and moistened with liquid manure, others a moist one, with a great deal of water.

Mr. Knight, of Hammersmith, has favoured us with his method of propagating it : during the summer, he ascertains the different varieties, which he keeps packed dry in sand, generally on the sides ; about the middle of January he removes them to a gentle heat, to forward their shoots, and when advanced to five or six inches in height, takes his cuttings, which he places in warm situations, by which plan he informs us he does not lose one in fifty, whereas were the cuttings taken in the summer or autumn, not one in fifty would take root ; he observes that great care must be taken to keep the plant perfectly dry when taken out of the ground, as the least moisture will at that time cause the roots to rot.

The Dahlia blossoms in July, and continues in bloom and beauty till late in the autumn; and when the weather has been mild, we have seen them boasting their autumnal splendour in December. It is said that the roots are good to eat, and in some degree resemble the Jerusalem artichoke; but we doubt its ever having been cultivated in our gardens except for its beauty.

Class, SYNGENESIA. *Order*, POLYGYNIA.

THE DAHLIA.

Though sever'd from its native clime,
   Where skies are ever bright and clear,
And nature's face is all sublime,
   And beauty clothes the fragrant air.
   The Dahlia will each glory wear,
With tints as bright, and leaves as green ;
And winter in his savage mien,
   May breathe forth storm,—yet she will bear
With all :—and in the summer ray,
. With blossoms deck the brow of day.

And thus the soul—if Fortune cast
   Its lot to live in scenes less bright,—
Should bloom amid the adverse blast ;—
   Nor suffer sorrow's clouds to blight
   Its outward beauty—inward light.
Thus should she live and flourish still,
Though misery's frosts might strive to kill
   The germ of hope within her quite :—
Thus should she hold each beauty fast,
And bud and blossom to the last.

WM. MARTIN.

EVENING PRIMROSE.

(*Ornothera.*)

THE Evening or Tree Primrose is a native of Virginia, and now common in most of our English gardens.

This delicately-coloured flower is usually shut during the day, as if to protect itself from the heat of the sun, but expands towards the approach of evening, whence it is called the Evening Primrose. It flowers in June, and continues for a considerable time in blossom.

There are three different sorts of this plant; but the most common in our gardens is the broad-leaved kind, with flat lance-shaped leaves, a hairy stalk and a corolla of pale yellow.

Class, OCTANDRIA.   *Order*, MONOGYNIA.

TO THE EVENING OR TREE PRIMROSE.

Fair flower, that shunn'st the glare of day,
    Yet lov'st to open, meekly bold,
To evening hues of sober grey,
    Thy cup of paly gold;

Be thine the offering, owing long
    To thee, and to this pensive hour,
Of one brief tributary song,
    Though transient as thy flower.

I love to watch, at silent eve,
    Thy scatter'd blossoms' lonely light;
And have my inmost heart receive
    The influence of that sight.

I love, at such an hour, to mark
    Their beauty greet the night-breeze chill,
And shine, 'mid shadows gathering dark,
    The garden's glory still.

For such, 'tis sweet to think the while,
    When cares and griefs the breast invade,
Is friendship's animating smile,
    In sorrow's dark'ning shade.

Thus it bursts forth, like thy pale cup,
   Glist'ning amid its dewy tears,
And bears the sinking spirit up,
   Amid its chilling fears.

But still more animating far,
   If meek Religion's eye may trace,
Even in thy glimm'ring earth-born star,
   The holier hope of grace !

The hope that, as thy beauteous bloom
   Expands to glad the close of day,
So through the shadows of thy tomb
   May break forth Mercy's ray.

BARTON.

THE EVENING PRIMROSE.

THERE are that love the shades of life,
   And shun the splendid walks of fame ;
There are that hold it rueful strife
   To risk Ambition's losing game.

That, far from Envy's lurid eye,
   The fairest fruits of Genius rear ;
Content to see them bloom and die
   In Friendship's small, but genial, sphere.

FLORA AND THALIA.

Than vainer flowers though sweeter far,
   The Evening Primrose shuns the day;
Blooms only to the western star,
   And loves its solitary ray.

In Eden's vale an aged hind,
   At the dim twilight's closing hour,
On his time-smoothed staff reclin'd,
   With wonder view'd the opening flower.

" Ill-fated flower, at eve to blow!"
   In pity's simple thought, he cries;
" Thy bosom must not feel the glow
   Of splendid suns, or smiling skies.

" Nor thee, the vagrants of the field,
   The hamlet's little train behold;
Their eyes to sweet oppression yield,
   When thine the falling shades unfold.

" Nor thee the hasty shepherd heeds,
   When love has filled his heart with cares;
For flowers he rifles all the meads,
   For waking flowers—but thine forbears.

" Ah! waste no more that beauteous bloom,
   On night's chill shade that fragrant breath;
Let smiling suns those gems illume!
   Fair flower, to live unseen is death!"

FABLES OF FLORA.

TO THE EVENING PRIMROSE.

FROM childhood I have lov'd thee more, pale flower,
   Than all the garden's gayest boast and pride;
For thine has ever been my fav'rite hour,
   The quiet, pensive, twilight eventide.

And I have watch'd thy beauteous leaves unfold,
   Soon as the sun has brightly sunk to rest,
Opening thy buds to meet the moonlight cold,
   And therefore 'twas, sweet flower, I lov'd thee
      best.

Memory, the moon, and thou, my friends have been,
   When other friends were scattered wide and far;
And now I value not night's brightest scene,
   If wanting thee, my chosen Evening Star.

                F. R. ELLIOTT.

FOXGLOVE.

(*Digitalis Purpurea.*)

THE Foxglove is perennial, commonly growing about road-sides and hedges, especially in dry gravelly soils; flowering in June and July. It is one of the most showy of our wild plants; and takes its name from the resemblance of the flower to the fingers of a glove. In a wild state it is purple, or red; when cultivated in gardens, white or yellow. Among the most deadly vegetable productions of this country, is the Foxglove, which,

> With modest blush in bosky dells,
> Hangs her dewy purple bells;
> So softly nodding in the breeze,
> The blossoms seldom fail to please;
> But woe to him who rashly sips,
> There's poison on her glowing lips!

Class, DIDYNAMIA.　*Order*, ANGIOSPERMIA.

F.

M. Spratt dc

THE FOXGLOVE AND THE HAREBELL.

In a valley obscure, on a bank of green shade,
A sweet little Harebell her dwelling had made;
Her roof was a woodbine, that tastefully spread
Its close-woven tendrils o'erarching her head;
Her bed was of moss, that each morning made new;
She dined on a sunbeam, and supp'd on the dew;
Her neighbour, the nightingale, sung her to rest;
And care had ne'er planted a thorn in her breast.

One morning she saw, on the opposite side,
A Foxglove displaying his colours of pride;
She gazed on his form that in stateliness grew,
And envied his height, and his brilliant hue;
She mark'd how the flow'rets all gave way before him,
While they pressed round her dwelling with far less
        decorum.
Dissatisfied, jealous, and peevish, she grows,
And the sight of the Foxglove destroys her repose;

She tires of her vesture, and swelling with spleen,
Cries, " Ne'er such a dowdy blue mantle was seen!"
Nor keeps to herself any longer her pain,
But thus to a primrose begins to complain:

"I envy your mood, that can patient abide
The respect paid that Foxglove, his airs and his p
There you sit, still the same, with your colo
    cheek,
But you have no spirit,—would I were as meek."

The Primrose, good-humour'd, replied, "If you kne
More about him (remember I'm older than you,
And, better instructed, can tell you his tale):
You'd envy him least of all flowers in the vale;
With all his fine airs and his dazzling show,
No blossom more baneful and odious can blow; ·
The reason that flow'rets before him give way
Is because they all hate him, and shrink from his
    ray.

"To stay near him long would be fading or death,
For he scatters a pest with his venomous breath;
While the flowers that you fancy are crowding you
    there,
Spring round you, delighted your converse to share.
His flame-colour'd robe is imposing, 'tis true,
Yet who likes it so well as your mantle of blue;
For we know that of innocence one is the vest,
The other the cloak of a treacherous breast.

"I see your surprise, but I know him full well,
And have number'd his victims, as fading they fell;
He blighted twin violets that under him lay,
And poisoned a sister of mine the same day."

M. Sprett. del.

The Primrose was silent—the Harebell, 'tis said,
Inclined for a moment her beautiful head;
But quickly recovered her spirits, and then
Declar'd that she ne'er should feel envy again.

ANON.

———

STOCK GILLIFLOWER.

(*Matthiola.*)

THE Gilliflower is a British plant, and well known to all who can procure a few yards of garden ground, being a hardy plant, and requiring little care and attention in its cultivation, although its beauty is much improved by the art and industry of the gardener; but, as botanists, we should never meddle with those that are double; they are deformed; nature will no longer be found among them; for, if the most brilliant part of the flower (the corolla) be multiplied, it is at the expense of the more essential parts, which disappear under this addition of brilliancy. In the single flowers we find the petals of the corolla standing wide from each other, forming a figure something like the cross of the order of St. Louis, whence these corollas are called cruciform, or cross-shaped. The Gilliflower is of almost all colours and hues; some are extremely beautiful; and the double sort has a brilliant appearance in

our flower-borders; the ten-week stock makes but
a poor show in comparison.

The smell is very agreeable, resembling, in a slight
degree, that of the clove pink.   It flowers in May.

Class, TETRADYNAMIA.   *Order*, SILIQUOSA.

TO THE MELANCHOLY GILLIFLOWER.

OH why, thou lone and lovely flower,
    Deny thy sweetness to the day;
And ever in night's hushest hour,
    Still sigh thy fragrant life away?

The wild bee murmurs round each spray,
    And kisses every flower but thine;
No scent allures the vagrant's way,
    Or tempts him to thy golden mine.

The glowing breath of gorgeous noon
    Is swelled by every other sweet;
Why dost thou only the pale moon
    And chilly night winds love to greet?

When young Endymion earliest dreamed,
    On that wild hill's enchanted ground,
The faltering radiance fearful gleamed,
    And cast a quivering light around.

Still, in his dreams, did charmed sighs
   Float trembling o'er his favoured head,
And strange mysterious music rise,
   And hover round his mountain bed.

Thine was the conscious flower, that threw
   Its lovely fragrance on the night;
Thou only oped thy pallid hue
   Beneath the silent flood of light.

Thy sisters veil their foreheads fair,
   And fold their bells on heath and dale;
Nor on the misty evening air
   Their breath of sweetness dare exhale.

But thou dost long for holy eve,
   To shroud thee from day's piercing eye;
Night's chilly hours alone receive
   Thy secret tear and perfumed sigh.

JUVENILE KEEPSAKE.

THE Melancholy Gilliflower, is a native of the sea coasts in the south of France, Spain, and Italy. Its blossoms, of a dull purple, are scentless in the day-time, but exhale a rich nocturnal fragrance.

F

LA GIROFLÉE.

MAIS quelle est cette fleur que son instinct pieux
Sur l'aile du Zephyr amène dans ces lieux?
Quoi ! tu quittes le temple ou vivent tes racines,
Sensible Giroflée, amante des ruines,
Et ton tribut fidèle accompagne nos rois ?
Ah ! puisque la terreur a courbé sous ses lois
Du lis infortuné sa liege souveraine,
Que nos jardins en deuil te choisissent pour reine;
Triomphe sans rivale, et que ta sainte fleur
Croisse pour le tombeau, le trône, et le malheur.

TRENEUIL.

LA GIROFLÉE.

Mais quelle est cette fleur que son instinct pieux
Sur l'aile du Zephyr amène dans ces lieux?
Quoi ! tu quittes le temple ou vivent tes racines,
Sensible Giroflée, amante des ruines,
Et ton tribut fidèle accompagne nos rois ?
Ah ! puisque la terreur a courbé sous ses lois
Du lis infortuné sa liege souveraine,
Que nos jardins en deuil te choisissent pour reine ;
Triomphe sans rivale, et que ta sainte fleur
Croisse pour le tombeau, le trône, et le malheur.

TRENEUIL.

HELIOTROPE, OR TURNSOLE.

(Heliotropium.)

THIS beautiful little plant a native of Peru, flowers in May; but in the greenhouse continues in bloom nearly all the year. It is said to turn to the sun, and thereby has acquired its name; but should a cloud obscure the sky, it droops its head. Its flowers are much esteemed for their beautiful simplicity and fragrance.

Class, PENTANDRIA. *Order*, MONOGYNIA.

THE HELIOTROPE.

THERE is a flower, whose modest eye
　Is turned with looks of light and love,
Who breathes her softest, sweetest sigh,
　Whene'er the sun is bright above.

Let clouds obscure, or darkness veil,
　Her fond idolatry is fled;
Her sighs no more their sweets exhale,
　The loving eye is cold and dead.

Canst thou not trace a moral here,
　False flatterer of the prosperous hour?
Let but an adverse cloud appear,
　And thou art faithless as the flow'r.

ANON.

I .

PURPLE IRIS.

(*Iris subbiflora.*)

THIS beautiful and showy plant is a native of Portugal, flowering in May; and from its height, the size of its blossoms, and the richness of its colours, it adds much to the splendour of the flower-garden, particularly in shady situations.

There are fifty-one species of Iris; from one of which is taken the beautiful perfume called orris root. The plant from which this is taken is a native of Italy, and was cultivated in England by Gerrard, in 1596; but the roots of the orris produced in this country, have neither the odour nor the other qualities of those from warmer climates.

Class, TRIANDRIA.   *Order*, MONOGYNIA.

THE IRIS * (OR RAINBOW).

How oft have I view'd thee, all glorious and bright,
In the pride of thy birth-place, thou vision of light;
Like an angel of gladness, in mercy design'd
As a token and herald of love to mankind!

There, too, where the floods of the desert resound,
Thou reignest unmoved by the tumult around;
And the eye may repose on thy soft smiling beams;
And the fancy may hail thee the Nymph of the streams.

Oh! thus, when the moments of sorrow are nigh,
When the stern voice of Nature shall call us to die;
At that thrilling hour, when, in anguish and pain,
Our spirits return to life's pleasure in vain;

May Peace with her soft silv'ry pinions be there,
To chase from our bosoms the phantom Despair.
May Hope, gentle Hope, with her sweetness illume
The darkness that shadows the depths of the tomb.

* The brilliancy of its colours, and the graceful curve of
its petals, emulate the arch of *Iris* or the rainbow.

JASMINE.

(*Jasminum.*)

THE white Jasmine is a native of China; and was first cultivated in England in the year 1549. From its beautiful blossom, fragrance of smell, and rapid growth, spreading its long pliable branches several feet in one summer, we find it a favourite plant for adorning verandas and summer-houses; and also for spreading along garden walls. Its numerous white flowers, intermingled with the dark green leaves, form a beautiful contrast.

There are several varieties: some being very large and double, and others yellow. At Malabar, the women string the larger double blossoms, and wear them round their necks for ornament, as well as for their odoriferous perfume: in our own country, the essence, extracted from the flowers, is much esteemed.

Class, DIANDRIA.   *Order*, MONOGYNIA.

JASMINE.

TO A FRIEND.

SWEET Jessamine, long may thy elegant flower,
  Breathe fragrance and solace to me ;
And long thy green sprigs overshadow the bower,
  Devoted to friendship and thee.

The eye that was dazzled, where lilies and roses
  Their brilliant assemblage display'd,
With grateful delight on thy verdure reposes,
  A tranquil and delicate shade.

But, ah ! what dejection thy foliage expresses,
  Which pensively droops on her breast ;
The dew of the evening has laden her tresses,
  And stands like a tear on her crest.

I'll watch by thy side through the gloom of the night,
  Impatient, till morning appears :
No charm can awaken this heart to delight,
  My Jasmine, while thou art in tears.

But soon will the shadows of night be withdrawn,
  Which ever in mercy are given ;
And thou shalt be cheered by the light of the morn,
  And fanned by the breezes of heaven.

And still may thy tranquil and delicate shade,
  Yield fragrance and solace to me;
For though all the flowers in my garden should fade,
  My heart will repose upon thee.

JANE TAYLOR.

ON THE INDIAN JASMINE FLOWER.

(*Jasminum Bignonia.*)

How lovelily the Jasmine flower
  Blooms far from man's observing eyes;
And having lived its little hour,
  There withers,—there sequestered dies.
Though faded, yet 'tis not forgot;
  A rich perfume time cannot sever,
Lingers in that unfriended spot,
  And decks the Jasmine's grave for ever.

Thus, thus should man, who seeks to soar,
  On Learning's wings, to Fame's bright sky,
Far from his fellows, seek that lore,
  Unheeded live, sequestered die.
Thus, like the Jasmine, when he's fled,
  Fame's rich perfume will ever keep,
Ling'ring around the faded dead,
  As saints that watch some infant's sleep.

R. RYAN.

TO THE JASMINE.

On gentle gales the grateful twilight came:
Dimpling the shining lakes, the fragrant breeze
Sighs o'er the lawns, and whispers thro' the trees.
Refreshed, the lily rears its silver head,
And opening Jasmines o'er the arbour spread.

CAMOENS.

'Twas midnight—through the lattice wreathed
With woodbine, many a perfume breathed
From plants that wake when others sleep;
From timid Jasmine-buds that keep
Their odour to themselves all day;
But when the sunlight dies away,
Let the delicious secret out
To every breeze that roams about.

MOORE.

JASMINE FLOWERS.

AND brides, as delicate and fair
As the white Jasmine flowers they wear,
  Hath Yemen in her blissful clime;
Who lulled in cool kiosk or bower,
  Before their mirrors count the time,
And grow still lovelier every hour.

MOORE.

TO A JASMINE TREE,

IN THE COURT OF HAWORTH CASTLE.

MY slight and slender Jasmine-tree,
  That bloomest on my border tower,
Thou art more dearly loved by me,
  Than all the wealth of fairy bower.
I ask not, while I near thee dwell,
  Arabia's spice or Syria's rose;
Thy light festoons more freshly smell,
  Thy virgin white more freshly glows.

My mild and winsome Jasmine-tree,
  That climbest up the dark grey wall,
Thy tiny flowerets seem in gloe,
  Like silver spray-drops, down to fall:

Say, did they from their leaves thus peep,
 When mailed moss-troopers rode the hill;
When helmed warders paced the keep,
 And bugles blew for Belted Will *?

My free and feathery Jasmine-tree,
 Within the fragrance of thy breath,
Yon dungeon grated to its key,
 And the chained captive pined for death.
On border fray, on feudal crime,
 I dream not while I gaze on thee;
The chieftains of that stern old time
 Could ne'er have loved a Jasmine-tree.

LORD MORPETH.

* Lord William Howard.—See " Lay of the Last
Minstrel," &c.

KING-CUP, OR, MEADOW CROWFOOT.

(*Ranunculus acris.*)

THIS is a perennial plant, and a native of meadows, and moist pastures, flowering in June and July; on being applied to the skin, it excites itching, redness, and inflammation, and even produces blisters; on being chewed it corrodes the tongue, and if taken into the stomach, brings on all the deleterious effects of an acrid poison. Mr. Curtis observes that even pulling up this plant and carrying it some little distance, excited considerable inflammation in the palm of the hand in which it was carried; but the acrimonious quality of this plant is completely dissipated by heat, and on its being thoroughly dried, becomes perfectly bland.

The flowers have, however, a pleasing appearance in our meadows, which they enamel with their bright yellow cups.

Class, POLYANDRIA. *Order*, POLYGYNIA.

G

TO THE KING-CUP.

Simple pledge of June's returning,
  Pleasing 'tis to see thy bloom,
Winter's rudest terrors spurning,
  Rising forth from nature's tomb.

Thy bright form betokens pleasure,
  When no piercing winds assail ;
June's creations, brightest treasure,
  Soon will breathe a sweeter gale.

Yet, bright flow'r, thy fate too often
  Emblem is of others' woe ;
When warm airs stern winter soften,
  Thy rich petals burst and blow.

But with sithe the mower hieing
  To the mead with anxious breath ;
Then around thee danger's flying,
  Then, bright flower, you sink in death.

So it is with human sorrow,
  Some dear friend smiles on our joy,
Anticipation cheers the morrow,
  Bliss feels then no dread alloy.

But alas ! stern sickness seizing,
  Sinks the sufferer to his doom ;
When the soul, with prospects pleasing,
  Mounts to joys beyond the tomb.

ALTERED FROM LACY'S PRIMROSE.

M. Spratt. del.

LAVENDER.

(*Lavandula spica.*)

This plant is perennial, and grows spontaneously in many of the southern parts of Europe, of which it is a native. It flowers from July to September, and from the fragrance of its blossom, is now so generally cultivated, that we can scarcely enter a garden where it is not to be found. To most people the perfume is agreeable, and the well-known Lavender water, so refreshing in a warm or crowded room, is made from its flowers. According to Dr. Cullen, Lavender is, when taken internally or applied externally, a powerful stimulant to the nervous system. The corollas of this plant are as it were turned topsy turvy, that which is the upperpart in most others being the lower in this, and vice versa: the calyces are supported by a bracte, and the stamens lie within the tube.

Class, DYDYNAMIA. *Order*, GYMNOSPERMIA.

"But know, that I a fragrance give—
  A fragrance that can never die;
E'en when my colours cease to live,
  My leaves that perfume shall supply."

Truly she spoke: the next day sees
  The fopling Poppy stripped and bare;
Its gaudy blooms are on the breeze,
  And tossed by every breath of air.

The Lavender still sweetly grew,
  Till Anne, one Summer morning, found,
By its rich fragrance where it grew;
  Its heads she plucked and gently bound.

But still it gives its matchless scent,
  Sweet as that maiden's spotless mind,
Which, when old age her charms has reft,
  Will charm by what is left behind.

R. PATTERSON.

Belfast.

M Spratt. del

MEZEREON.

(*Daphne mezereum.*)

THIS beautiful and hardy shrub is a native of England, and is found growing wild in the woods near Andover, in Hampshire, and about Laxfield, in Suffolk. The colour of their blossoms varies in hue from deep red to peach-coloured and white.

This shrub, which is valued for visiting us when few others are in bloom, flowers in February and March; the blossoms surround the stem, and the leaves, which are lance-shaped, appear at the terminations of the branches after the flowers are expanded.

There is a different sort found wild in woods and shady hedges, called spurge laurel, (*Daphne laureola*,) which is evergreen; but it will not bear a comparison with the *Daphne mezereum*, the corollas being of a dingy green, and not having the agreeable odour of that more beautiful shrub. The germen, which is oval, becomes a beautiful red berry, and is said to be poisonous both to man and beast, but birds eat freely of it.

Class, OCTANDRIA. *Order*, MONOGYNIA.

ON RECEIVING A BRANCH OF MEZEREON,

WHICH FLOWERED AT WOODSTOCK, DECEMBER, 1803.

ODOURS of spring, my sense ye charm
   With fragrance premature,
And, 'mid these days of dark alarm,
   Almost to hope allure.
Methinks with purpose soft ye came,
   To tell of brighter hours,
Of May's blue skies, abundant bloom,
   Her sunny gales and showers.

Alas! for me shall May in vain
   The powers of life restore;
These eyes, that weep and watch in pain,
   Shall see her charms no more.
No, no, this anguish cannot last!
   Beloved friends, adieu!
The bitterness of death were past,
   Could I resign but you.

     *   *   *   *   *   *

Oh ye ! who soothe the pangs of death
   With love's own patient care,
Still, still retain this fleeting breath,
   Still pour the fervent prayer.
And ye, whose smile must greet my eye
   No more, nor voice my ear,
Who breathe for me the tender sigh,
   And shed the pitying tear;

Whose kindness (though far, far removed)
   My grateful thoughts perceive;
Pride of my life—esteemed, beloved,
   My last sad claim receive !
Oh do not quite your friend forget—
   Forget alone her faults;
And speak of her with fond regret,
   Who asks your lingering thoughts.

MRS. TIGHE.

NARCISSUS.

(*Narcissus Tasetta.*)

THIS beautiful and fragrant flower is a native of Northern India, of China, and Japan. Sir James Smith informs us that it decorated in profusion the banks of the Alpheus; even the barbarians had taste enough to collect nosegays of those lovely flowers. The appearance of this elegantly formed flower, so early in the season, we hail with more pleasure because it is almost among the first to welcome the approach of spring. The colour of the corolla varies; some being white, with a deep yellow cup edged with red; others pale primrose; and some entirely of a bright yellow. By the art of cultivation, the florists have produced a very fine variety with double petals in the corolla.

Class, HEXANDRIA. *Order*, MONOGYNIA.

N.

M. Spratt

TO THE NARCISSUS.

ARISE, and speak thy sorrows, Echo, rise;
Here, by this fountain, where thy love did pine,
Whose memory lives fresh to vulgar fame,
Shrined in this yellow flower, that bears his name.

ECHO.—His name revives, and lifts me up from earth,—
See, see, the mourning fount, whose springs weep yet
Th' untimely fate of that too beauteous boy,
That trophy of self-love, and spoil of nature,
Who (now transformed into this drooping flower)
Hangs the repentant head back from the stream;
As if it wished,—would I had never looked
In such a flattering mirror! O Narcissus!
Thou that wast once (and yet art) my Narcissus,
Had Echo but been private with thy thoughts,
She would have dropt away herself in tears,
Till she had all turned water, that in her
(As in a truer glass) thou might'st have gaz'd,
And seen thy beauties by more kind reflection.
But self-love never yet could look on truth,
But with bleared beams; slick Flattery and she
Are twin-born sisters, and do mix their eyes,
As, if you sever one, the other dies.

Why did the gods give thee a heavenly form,
And earthly thoughts to make thee proud of it?
Why do I ask?   'Tis now the known disease
That Beauty hath, to bear too deep a sense
Of her own self-conceived excellence.
O hadst thou known the worth of heaven's rich gift,
Thou wouldst have turned it to a truer use,
And not (with starved and covetous ignorance)
Pined in continual eyeing that bright gem
The glance whereof to others had been more,
Than to thy famished mind, the wide world's store.

BEN JONSON.

THE NARCISSUS.

HERE young Narcissus o'er the fountain stood,
And viewed his image in the crystal flood;
The crystal flood reflects his lovely charms,
And the pleased image strives to meet his arms.
No nymph his unexperienced breast subdued,
Echo in vain the flying boy pursued.
Himself alone, the foolish youth admires,
And with fond look the smiling shade desires;
O'er the smooth lake with fruitless tears he grieves;
His spreading fingers shoot in verdant leaves;
Through his pale veins green sap now gently flows,
And in a short lived flow'r his beauty blows.

M. Spratt.

Let vain Narcissus warn each female breast,
That beauty's but a transient good at best;
Like flow'rs it withers with th' advancing year,
And age like winter robs the blooming fair.

GAY.

ORCHIS.

(*Orchis.*)

THIS plant, which is common in meadows, is a perennial, flowering in April and May.

There are no less than fifty different species of the Orchis; which, seeming to spurn culture and art, are not capable of essential changes, except in the colour of the flowers; and they require to be examined to see all their beauty. For this purpose we should seek for them abroad in the meadows; and one of the great advantages of botany is, that we must add exercise to study, as we cannot learn it from books, sitting in our easy chair by the fire-side. The root is gelatinous, and possesses the same qualities as gum arabic. The saloop, which is imported here from the east, and was formerly held in great estimation, is now well known to be a preparation of the Orchis roots.

Mr. Mault has recommended a method of preparing them; and his specimens of salep were equal, if not superior, to that brought from the Levant: it is as follows:—

H

" The root is to be washed in water, and the fine brown skin which covers it to be separated by means of a small brush, dipping the roots in hot water, and rubbing them with a coarse linen cloth; when cleansed, they are to be spread upon tin, and placed in an oven heated as for bread; there they are to remain six or ten minutes, by which time they will have lost their milky whiteness, and have acquired a transparency like horn, without any diminution of bulk; they are then to be removed, to dry and harden in the air, which will require several days. Saloop, considered as an article of diet, is extremely nutritious, containing a great quantity of farinaceous matter in a small bulk; and hence it was thought fit to constitute it a part of ships' provisions, to prevent famine at sea; for it is asserted by Dr. Percival that one ounce of this saloop, and the same quantity of portable soup, dissolved in two quarts of boiling water, will be sufficient sustenance for one man a day.   The Romans believed it to be the food of the satyrs; hence the name *Orchis Satyrium.*

Class, GYNANDRIA.   *Order,* DIANDRIA.

THE ORCHIS.

See, Delia, see this image bright;
Why starts my fair one at the sight?
It mounts not on obtrusive wing,
Nor threats thy breast with angry sting;
Admire, as close the insect lies,
Its thin-wrought plume and honey'd thighs;
Whilst on this flow'ret's velvet breast
It seems as though 'twere lull'd to rest,
Nor might its fairy wings unfold,
Enchain'd in aromatic gold.
Think not to set the captive free—
'Tis but the picture of a bee.

Yet wonder not that Nature's power
Should paint an insect in a flower,
And stoop to means that bear in part
Resemblance to imperfect art.
Nature, who could that form inspire
With strength and swiftness, life and fire,
And bid it search each spicy vale,
Where flowers their fragrant souls exhale;
And labouring for the parent hive,
With murmurs make the wild alive.

H 2

For when in Parian stone we trace
Some best-remember'd form or face ;
Or see on radiant canvas rise
An imitative paradise ;
And feel the warm affections' glow,
Pleased at the pencil's mimic show ;
'Tis but obedience to the plan
From Nature's birth proposed to man ;
Who, lest her choicest sweets in vain
Should blossom for our thankless train ;
Lest beauty pass unheeded by,
Like cloud upon the summer sky ;
Lest mem'ry of the brave and just,
Should sleep with them consign'd to dust ;
With leading hand th' expedient proves,
And paints for us the form she loves.

R. SNOW, ESQ.

M. Spratt. del

CLOVE PINK.

(Dianthus Caryophillus.)

THIS fragrant plant is perennial, and grows wild in several parts of England, in old walls and in crevices of rocks (at Rochester, Deal, Sandown, and other castles, plentifully) : but the choicest kinds are cultivated in our gardens, where they become extremely luxuriant; and by the aid of culture, that beautiful variety is raised, so highly esteemed under the name of Carnation; and which is universally acknowledged a worthy leader of one of the finest natural orders. When we consider the size of the flower, the beauty of its colour, the arrangement of its parts, and, above all, the singularly rich and spicy odour that it exhales, we cannot withhold that tribute of admiration which will ever be given it. For ornament and beauty, we should gather these flowers from the parterre; but as botanists, we should take them from a wall, or a dry untilled soil, where their simplicity, and the clearness of their natural character, will make amends for their want of splendour.

Class, DECANDRIA.   *Order*, DIGYNIA.

PINKS AND CARNATIONS.

Stay while ye will, or goe,
   And leave no scent behind ye;
Yet, trust me, I shall know
   The place where I may find ye.
Within my Lucia's cheek, .
   (Whose livery ye wear)
Play ye at hide or seeke,
   I'm sure to find ye there.

HERRICK.

So smell those odours that do rise
From out the wealthy spiceries;
So smells the flower of blooming clove,
Or roses smothered in the stove;
So smells the air of spiced wine,
Or essences of jessamine;
So smells the breath about the hives,
When well the work of honey thrives,
And the busic factours come
Laden with wax and honey home;

So smell those neat and woven bowers,
All over arched with orange-flowers,
And almond-blossoms that do mix,
To make rich these aromatics;
Thus sweet she smells; oh! what can be
More liked by her, or loved by me?

                                        HERRICK.

The warden of these haughty towers
    Has reared me into day;
And well the proud carnation's flowers,
    The cares of man repay.
In Flora's thousand glories drest,
    My varied petals bloom,
And well the loaded gales attest,
    Their burdens of perfume.

                FROM THE GERMAN OF GOETHE.

QUINCE.

(Pyrus Cydonia.)

THIS tree, which seldom rises very high, being usually crooked and distorted, appears originally to have been brought from Cydon, in Crete; hence the name Cydonia. At present the Quince grows wild upon the banks of the Danube, though in a much less luxuriant state than in our British gardens. The delicate pink blossoms of this tree, add much to the beautiful appearance of our orchards; and the flavour of its fruit is too well known to need any comment.

Class, ICOSANDRIA.   *Order,* PENTAGYNIA.

M. Spratt del.

THE QUINCE TREE.

I HAD a little comely cot,
  As neat as cottage well could be;
And near it rose a garden-plot,
  Where flourished one delightful tree;
  Ah! 'twas a tree of trees to me!

Its crooked branches o'er my head,
  Waved wide, an arched canopy;
And its bright leaves benignly spread
  A fan of green embroidery,
  That shaded all my family.

It was a screen from wind or sun,
  A veil from curiosity;
And when its summer bloom was gone,
  We still could feast with social glee,
  On its autumnal fruitery.

E'en Winter oft has seen it gay,
  With fretted frost-work spangled o'er;
While pendants drooped from every spray,
  And crimson budlets told once more,
  That Spring would all its charms restore!

But I have left that comely cot,
    Where blossoms now my favourite tree !
And I possess an ampler spot,
    Which boasts of more variety,
    And more enraptures all but me.

ALTERED FROM PARK'S FILBERT TREE.

PROVENCE, or HUNDRED-LEAVED ROSE.

(*Rosa centifolia.*)

THIS elegant species of rose-bush, a native of Europe, was first cultivated in England in the year 1596. According to the Hortus Cantabrigiensis, there are fifty-eight species of the Rose, of which the moss rose is perhaps the most beautiful. This species rises in our English gardens from four to five feet; but in Persia it grows to much greater perfection. Many of the roses, though so much cultivated in our gardens, are far from being distinctly characterised; those denominated varieties are extremely numerous, and often permanently uniform; and the specific differences are, in many respects, so inadequate to the purpose of satisfactory discrimination, that it becomes difficult to say which are varieties only.

In no part of the world is the rose so much esteemed as in Persia, where they hold a festival in honour of this flower.

M. Spratt del.

Rose! thou art the sweetest flower
That ever drank the amber shower;
Rose! thou art the fondest child
Of dimpled Spring, and wood-nymph wild:
Even the gods, who walk the sky,
Are amorous of thy scented sigh.

MOORE.

The *rosa canina*, or dog rose, which adorns our hedges in the summer, bears the fruit known by the name of heps, of which the well-known conserve is made.

Class, ICOSANDRIA.   *Order*, POLYGYNIA.

LOVE IN A ROSE-BUD.

A FRAGMENT.

As late each flower that sweetest blows
  I plucked, the garden pride;
Within the petals of a Rose
  A sleeping Love I spied.

Around his brows a beamy wreath
  Of many a lucent hue;
All purple glowed his cheek beneath,
  Inebriate with dew.

COLERIDGE.

A THOUGHT OF THE ROSE.

Rosa, Rosa ! perche sulla tua beltà,
Sempre è scritta questa parola—Morte ?

How much of memory dwells amidst thy bloom,
   Rose ! ever wearing beauty for thy dower!
The bridal day—the festival—the tomb—
   Thou hast thy part in each, thou stateliest flower!

Therefore, with thy soft breath, come floating by
   A thousand images of love and grief;
Dreams, filled with tokens of mortality ;
   Deep thoughts of all things beautiful and brief.

Not such thy spell o'er those who hailed thee first,
   In the clear light of Eden's golden day ;
There thy rich leaves to crimson glory burst,
   Linked with no dim remembrance of decay.

Rose ! for the banquet gathered, and the bier ;
   Rose ! coloured now by human hope or pain ;
Surely where death is not, nor change, nor fear,
   Yet we may meet thee, joy's own flower, again.

                 MRS. HEMANS.

THE LAST ROSE OF SUMMER.

'Tis the last Rose of summer
  Left blooming alone,
All her lovely companions
  Are faded and gone ;
No flower of her kindred,
  No rose-bud is nigh,
To reflect back her blushes,
  And give sigh for sigh.

I'll not leave thee, thou lone one,
  To pine on the stem ;
Since the lovely are sleeping,
  Go, sleep thou with them.
Thus kindly I scatter
  Thy leaves on the bed,
Where thy mates of the garden
  Lie scentless and dead.

So soon may I follow,
  When friendships decay,
And from love's shining circle
  The gems drop away ;
When true hearts lie withered,
  And fond ones are flown,
Oh ! who would inhabit
  This cold world alone ?

T. MOORE.

I

SURE THE ROSE IS LIKE A SIGH.

COMPOSED BY A BLIND CHILD.

If this delicious grateful flower,
Which blooms but for a little hour,
Should to the sight as lovely be
As from its fragrance seems to me,
A sigh must then its colour show,
For that's the softest joy I know.
And sure the Rose is like a sigh,
Born just to soothe, and then to die.

My father, when our fortune smiled,
With jewels decked his sightless child ;
Their glittering worth the world might see,
But ah ! they shed no sweets for me !
Still as the present failed to charm,
The trickling drops bedew'd my arm ;
And sure the gem to me most dear,
Was a kind father's pitying tear

THE ROSE.

As through a garden late I roved,
    And musing walked along,
While list'ning to the blackbird's note,
    Or linnet's cheerful song ;

Around were flowers of various hues ;
    The pink and daisy pied ;
When, in the centre of a grove,
    A blushing rose I spied.

Eager to pluck the beauteous flower,
    I quickly hastened there ;
Securely in my bosom placed,
    And watched with tender care.

Its fragrant odours grateful were,
    And pleasant to the sense ;
Its leaves with brightest colours glowed
    Like virgin innocence.

But, lo, ere evening dews descend,
    Those beauteous tints were fled ;
Withered and blasted in their prime,
    And drooped its tow'ring head.

Sweet blossom! then I sighing said,
  How soon thy beauties die;
The fairest flower the garden knows,
  With thee in vain would vie.

Be thou my silent monitor,
  And warn my heedless youth,
The graces of the mind to seek,
  In piety and truth.

For outward charms of shape or face
  Soon wither, like the rose;
But virtue, lovely e'en in death,
  Fresh beauties will disclose.

ORIGINAL.

THE YOUNG ROSE.

The young Rose which I gave thee, so dewy and bright,
Was the flow'ret most dear to the sweet bird of night;
Who oft by the moon o'er her blushes hath hung,
And thrilled every leaf with the wild lay he sung.

Oh! take, then, this young Rose, and let her life be,
Prolonged by her breath she will borrow from thee!
For while o'er her bosom thy soft notes shall thrill,
She'll think the sweet night-bird is courting her still.

A ROSE-BUD BY MY EARLY WALK.

A ROSE-BUD, by my early walk,
Adown a corn-inclosed bawk,
Sae gently bent its thorny stalk,
    All on a dewy morning.
Ere twice the shades o' dawn are fled,
In a' its crimson glory spread,
And drooping rich the dewy head,
    It scents the early morning.
Within the bush, her covert nest
A little linnet fondly prest,
The dew sat chilly on her breast
    Sae early in the morning.
She soon shall see her tender brood
The pride, the pleasure o' the wood,
Amang the fresh green leaves bedew'd,
    Awake the early morning.
So thou, dear bird, young Jeany fair,
On trembling string, or vocal air,
Shall sweetly pay the tender care
    That tents thy early morning.
So thou, sweet Rose-bud, young and gay,
Shalt beauteous blaze upon the day,
And bless the parent's evening ray,
    That watch'd thy early morning.

                                    BURNS.

I 3

THE ROSE OF SUMMER.

CHILD of the Summer, charming Rose,
   No longer in confinement lie;
Arise to light, thy form disclose,
   Rival the spangles of the sky.

The rains are gone, the storms are o'er,
   Winter retires to make thee way:
Come, then, thou sweetly-blushing flow'r,
   Come, lovely stranger, come away.

The sun is dress'd in beaming smiles,
   To give thy beauties to the day;
Young zephyrs wait with gentle gales,
   To fan thy bosom as they play.

                CASSIMIR.

THE DOG ROSE.

THE rose is fairest when 'tis budding new,
And hope is brightest when it dawns from fears;
The rose is sweetest washed with morning dew,
And love is loveliest when embalmed in tears.
O, wilding Rose, whom fancy thus endears,
I bid your blossoms in my bonnet wave,
Emblem of hope and love through future years.

             LADY OF THE LAKE.

THE MOSS-ROSE.

(*Rosa muscosa.*)

THE Rosebud swelled in Sharon's vale,
  And bloom'd in Eden beauteously,
It drank the breath of southern gale,
  It prov'd the warmth of summer sky ;
But o'er thy growth no summer rose,
But drifted lay the untrodden snows.

The Rose of England beamed of yore,
  In lily and in crimson hue ;
Its bloom was dipped in human gore,
  And sullied were its leaves to view;
Bnt thou hast spread amidst the storm,
In stainless purity thy form.

Sweet innocence ! by mercy fed,
  With light, and warmth, and shelter meet ;
Whilst winter all his horrors sped,
  In drifted snow and driving sleet ;
Thus have I seen, in maiden form,
A beauteous nursling of the storm !

Sweet purity ! no grosser breath
  Of fervid winds and scorching skies,
Taught thee to spring from mother earth,
  And, midst impurities arise;
But thou hast sprung a lovely thing,
Nor proved the genial breath of Spring.

Sweet messenger of triumph due,
  O'er death in all his wintry pride,
He cannot quench one living hue,
  Which Heaven has destined to abide,
Undimm'd 'midst Nature's dire decay,
To blossom in eternal day.

I'll fix thee here beside my heart,
  To calm its pulse, and check its play,
To heal its wounds, and soothe its smart,
  And chase the rankling thought away;
For surely nought of earthly care,
May mar its peace when thou art there.

                              GILLESPIE.

Oh, sooner shall the Rose of May
  Mistake her own sweet nightingale,
And to some newer minstrel's lay,
  Open her bosom's glowing veil *,
Than love shall ever doubt a tone,
A breath of the beloved one.

                              MOORE.

  * A frequent image among Oriental poets.

THE MOSS-ROSE.

THE Angel of the Flowers, one day,
Beneath a rose-tree sleeping lay;
That spirit to whom charge is given,
To bathe young buds in dews of heaven;
Awaking from his light repose,
The Angel whispered to the Rose:—
" O, fondest object of my care,
Still fairest found, where all is fair;
For the sweet shade thou giv'st to me,
Ask what thou wilt, 'tis granted thee !"
" Then," said the Rose, with deepened glow,
" On me another grace bestow."
The spirit paused in silent thought;—
What grace was there the flower had not?—
'Twas but a moment—o'er the Rose
A veil of moss, the Angel throws;
And robed in nature's simplest weed,
Could there a flower that Rose exceed?

FROM THE GERMAN.

THE MOSS-ROSE.

In the garden of Venus a Moss-rose grew,
    As sweet as a morning in May;
But the sunbeams had drank all her exquisite dew,
    And left her, alas! to decay.
A Zephyr, who long in his covert had lain,
    As the twilight advancing stole out,
He danced with the Gossamers over the plain,
    And fanned them in ether about.
He saw the Rose drooping, as nearer he flew,
    And skipped round her withering stem;
The soft air of evening over her blew,
    And decked her with many a gem.
As lovely again did appear the Moss-rose,
    As when in her earlier bloom;
And to Zephyr she gave, as she sank to repose,
    All the sweets of her luscious perfume.

                                   T. B.

THE ROSE.

AN IDYLL *.

SAID Ino, " I prefer the Rose
To every radiant flower that blows;
For when the smiling seasons fly,
And winds and rain deform the sky,
And roses lose their vivid bloom,
Their leaves retain a sweet perfume.
Emblem of virtue! virtue stays
When beauty's transient hue decays;
Nor age, nor fortune's frown efface,
Or injure her inherent grace."
" True," answered Daphnis; " but observe,
Unless some careful hand preserve
The leaves, before their tints decay,
They fall neglected; blown away
By wintry winds or beating rains,
No breath of fragrancy remains.
Some kindly hand must interpose;
For sore the wintry tempest blows,
And weak and delicate's the Rose."

RICHARDSON.

* The Idyll, or Idyllion, seems to signify, according to
the practice of the ancients, a representation in verse,
most commonly of some pastoral or rural incident.

TO MY BELOVED DAUGHTER.

THE Rose that hails the morning,
    Arrayed in all its sweets,
Its mossy couch adorning,
    The sun enamoured meets;
Yet when the warm beam rushes,
    Where, hid in gloom, it lies,
O'erwhelmed with glowing blushes,
    The hapless victim dies.

Sweet maid, this Rose discovers
    How frail is beauty's doom,
When flattery round it hovers,
    To spoil its proudest bloom:
Then shun each gaudy pleasure,
    That lures thee on to fade,
And guard thy beauty's treasure
    To decorate a shade.

                        MARY ROBINSON.

ON THE ROSE.

YE violets, that first appear,
    By your pure purple mantles known,
Like the proud virgins of the year,
    As if the spring were all your own—
    What are ye when the Rose is blown?

                        SIR H. WOTTON.

ON THE OPENED ROSE.

Oh mark those smiling tears, that swell
The opened Rose : from heaven they fell,
  And with the sunbeams blend ;
Blest visitations from above,
Such are the tender woes of love,
  Fostering the heart they bend.

S. T. COLERIDGE.

ON THE SAME.

Yon viewless wanderer of the vale,
The spirit of the western gale,
At morning's break, at evening's close,
Inhales the sweetness of the Rose ;
And hovers o'er the uninjured bloom,
Sighing back the soft perfume ;
Vigour to the zephyr's wing,
Her nectar-breathing kisses fling ;
And he the glitter of the dew,
Scatters on the Rose's hue.
Bashful, lo ! she bends her head,
And darts a blush of deeper red !

S. T. COLERIDGE.

K

THE ROSE-BUD.

BEAUTEOUS Rose-bud, young and gay,
Blooming in the early May;
Never mayst thou, lovely flow'r,
Chilly shrink in sleety show'r!
Never Boreas' hoary path,
Never Eurus' pois'nous breath,
Never baleful stellar lights,
Taint thee with untimely blights!
Never, never, reptile thief,
Riot on thy virgin leaf!
Not even Sol too fiercely view
Thy bosom blushing still with dew!
Mayst thou long, sweet crimson gem,
Richly deck thy native stem;
Till some ev'ning, sober, calm,
Dropping dews, and breathing balm,
While all around the woodland rings,
And ev'ry bird thy requiem sings;
Thou, amid the dirgeful sound,
Shed thy dying honours round,
And resign to parent earth,
The loveliest form she e'er gave birth.

BURNS.

SOLOMON'S SEAL.

(*Convallaria polygonatum.*)

THIS plant is perennial, and a native of Britain, growing in rocky and woody parts, and flowering in May and June. The root is beset with knobs, and marked with circular depressions, resembling the impression of a seal; hence it has acquired the name " Solomon's Seal."

In Galen's time this plant was much used by ladies to remove freckles, and for beautifying the skin. The berries, flowers, and leaves, are said to be poisonous.

Class, HEXANDRIA.   *Order*, MONOGYNIA.

K 2

TO SOLOMON'S SEAL.

White bud! that in meek beauty so dost lean,
  Thy cloistered cheek as pale as moonlight snow,
Thou seem'st beneath thy large high leaf of green,
  An eremite beneath his mountain's brow.
White bud! thou'rt emblem of a lovetide thing,
  The broken spirit that'its anguish bears
To silent shades; and there sits offering
  To heaven the holy fragrance of its tears.

ANON.

Sweet flower, you fondly strive to hide
  Your lovely form from public view,
While the gay blossom's eastern pride
  Appears in every varied hue.

So will a cultur'd feeling mind,
  Oft trembling shrink from worldly gaze;
Whilst flippant wit, at ease reclined,
  Spreads all around its transient rays.

Yet do I love that modest flower,
  Which blossoms in the humble shade,
And asks not for the sun's bright power,
  By which this splendid plant's arrayed.

ANON.

SPARE MY FLOWER.

OH spare my flower, my gentle flower,
  The slender creature of a day!
Let it bloom out its little hour,
            And pass away.
Too soon its fleeting charms must lie
  Decayed, unnoticed, overthrown;
O, hasten not its destiny,
            Too like thy own.

The breeze will roam this way tomorrow,
  And sigh to find its playmate gone :
The bee will come its sweets to borrow,
              And meet with none.
O spare ! and let it still outspread
  Its beauties to the passing eye,
And look up from its lowly bed,
            Upon the sky.

O spare my flower ! thou know'st not what
  Thy undiscerning hand would tear ;
A thousand charms thou notest not,
              Lie treasured there.

K 3

Not Solomon, in all his state,
  Was clad like Nature's simplest child ;
Nor could the world combined create
      One flow'ret wild.

Spare, then, this humble monument
  Of an Almighty's power and skill ;
And let it at his shrine present
      Its homage still.
He made it, who made nought in vain :
  He watches it, who watches thee ;
And He can best its date ordain,
      Who bade it be.

O spare my flower ! for it is frail,
  A timid, weak, imploring thing—
And let it still upon the gale,
      Its moral fling.
That moral thy reward shall be :
  Catch the suggestion, and apply—
" Go live like me," it cries; " like me
      " Soon, soon, to die."

REV. F. H. LYTE.

M. Spratt. del

TOBACCO.

(*Nicotiana Tabacum.*)

TOBACCO is a native of America, and was first imported into Europe about the middle of the sixteenth century, by Hermandez de Toledo, who sent it to Spain and Portugal. At that time the ambassador of Francis II. resided at the Court of Lisbon; and in the year 1560 he carried the tobacco into France, when it was presented to Catherine de Medicis, as a plant from the New World, possessing extraordinary virtues; the ambassador's name was Nicot, from whence it has taken the name Nicotiana.

The tobacco is an annual plant, flowering in July and August, and is now common in various parts of the globe; it is frequently used medicinally, although proved to be a deleterious poison. The fume of it is often applied to destroy the insects on plants in greenhouses and conservatories, and also to keep moths from woollen cloths and furs.

Class, PENTANDRIA. *Order*, MONOGYNIA.

THE TOBACCO PLANT.

How short-lived the struggle for honour or power,
Of the brightest rosebud, or more fragrant flower,
Who claim for their form, or their beauty alone,
Their right to be placed on the garden throne ;
A form without blemish may strike the sight,
Or fragrance alone the senses delight ;
But I have been prized for my virtues I ween,
And was once quite beloved by an *English queen* * ;
No disdain, then, I fear, nor from beauty a frown,
Since the worth of *Tobacco* was owned by a crown.
How can the gay tulip, then, e'er think to claim,
From the labour of poets such honour or fame ;
Or the poor lowly violet, the offspring of chance,
While I am esteemed both in Holland and France ;
To visit the nobles I've crossed the *Great Line* ;
I'm prized in all climates, such virtues are mine.
Those honours I gain for my perfume alone ;
True worth will be valued when beauty has flown.

* Queen Charlotte, consort of George III. was very partial
to snuff.

M. Spratt. del.

THE UVA-URSI, OR BEAR BERRY.

THE Uva-Ursi is perennial, a native of the northern parts of Britain, and flowers in June; it grows in different parts of Europe and America in great abundance, particularly in sandy soils. This beautiful plant, though formerly employed by the ancients as a remedy for many diseases, has almost entirely fallen into disuse, except as an ornament in our green-houses: the delicacy of its blossoms, grouped together at the top of each branch, is not excelled by any flower that graces the conservatory, or green-house.

Class, DECANDRIA.   *Order*, MONOGYNIA.

TO THE UVA-URSI.

How modest, sweet, and bright,
  Your clust'ring flow'rs appear ;
Above the leaves to hail the light,
  And meet the sunshine there.

But when the summer's sun is sped,
  Where will your bloom be found ;
Your blossoms gone, your leaves all dead.
  And scattered on the ground.

Yet when next June's bright sun is high,
  Your modest flow'rs will spring
In all their beauty to the sky,
  And leaves around you bring.

Just such is youth of virtuous breast,
  He'll fade but yet to bloom ;
And in his Saviour's bosom rest,
  When risen from the tomb.

ANON.

VIOLET PANSEY, or THREE-COLOURED VIOLET.

(*Viola tricolor.*)

THIS plant grows wild in corn fields, waste, and cultivated grounds; flowering all the summer, it varies much by culture, and from the variety of its colours, often becomes extremely beautiful in our gardens.

There are now twenty different coloured violets, or heartsease, cultivated by our florists.

This flower, the universal favourite of the more simple unrefined ages, is one of those in which, when we compare the diminutive and almost colourless pansy, which we find wild among the corn, with the ample rich-coloured corolla and its tissue of velvet, as is now common in many gardens, we cannot but allow that human art has made a considerable improvement; and we survey it with more pleasure, because it is not at the expense of the natural characters of the flower.

This violet has numerous provincial names, all bearing some allusion to love; perhaps the most universal is that of heartsease.

Class, PENTANDRIA: *Order*, MONOGYNIA.

THE VIOLET.

WHY better than the lady rose,
  Love I this little flower?
Because its fragrant leaves are those
  I loved in childhood's hour.

Though many a flower may win my praise,
  The violet has my love;
I did not pass my childish days
  In garden or in grove.

My garden was the window-seat,
  Upon whose edge was set
A little vase,—the fair, the sweet,
  It was the violet.

It was my pleasure and my pride;
  How I did watch its growth!
For health and bloom what plans I tried,
  And often injured both.

I placed it in the summer shower,
  I placed it in the sun;
And ever at the evening hour
  My work seemed half undone.

The broad leaves spread, the small buds grew,
  How slow they seemed to be,
At last there came a tinge of blue,
  'Twas worth the world to me.

At length the perfume fill'd the room,
  Shed from their purple wreath;
No flower has now so rich a bloom,
  Has now so sweet a breath.

I gathered two or three,—they seemed
  Such rich gifts to bestow;
So precious in my sight, I deemed
  That all must think them so.

Ah! who is there but would be fain
  To be a child once more;
If future years could bring again
  All that they brought before!

My heart's world has been long o'erthrown,
  It is no more of flowers;
Their bloom is past, their breath is flown,
  Yet I recal those hours.

Let nature spread her loveliest,
  By spring or summer nurst;
Yet still I love the violet best,
  Because I loved it first.

MISS LANDON.

L

LE VIOLE.

Non di verdi giardin, ornati e colti,
  Del soave e dolce acre Pestano,
  Veniam Madonna nella tua bianca mano;
Ma in aspre selve, e valli ombrose colti
Ove Venere afflitta, e in pensier molti
  Pel periglio d'Adon, correndo in vano,
  Un spino acuto al nudo piè villano
Sparse del divin sangue i boschi folti;
Noi sommettimmo allore il bianco fiore,
  Tanto che 'l divin sangue non aggiunge
A terra, ond' il color purpureo nacque.
  Non aure estive o vivi tolti a lunge,
Noi nutrit' anno, ma sospir d'amore
L'aure son sute, e pianti d'Amore l'acque.

                    LORENZO DE MEDICI.

HEARTSEASE.

(*Viola tricolor.*)

I USED to love thee, simple flower,
　To love thee dearly when a boy;
For thou didst seem, in childhood's hour,
　The smiling type of childhood's joy.

But now thou only mock'st my grief,
　By waking thoughts of pleasures fled.
Give me—give me the withered leaf,
　That falls on Autumn's bosom dead.

For that ne'er tells of what has been,
　But warns me what I soon shall be;
It looks not back on pleasure's scene,
　But points unto futurity.

I love thee not, thou simple flower,
　For thou art gay, and I am lone;
Thy beauty died with childhood's hour—
　The Heart's-ease from my path is gone.

　　　　　　　LONDON MAGAZINE.

LOVE-IN-IDLENESS.

In gardens oft a beauteous flower there grows,
    By vulgar eyes unnoticed and unseen ;
In sweet security it humbly blows,
    And rears its purple head to deck the green.

This flower, as Nature's poet sweetly sings,
    Was once milk-white, and Heart's-ease was its name,
Till wanton Cupid poised its roseate wings,
    A vestal's sacred bosom to inflame.

With treacherous aim the god his arrow drew,
    Which she with icy coldness did repel ;
Rebounding thence with feathery speed it flew,
    Till on this lonely flower, at last, it fell.

Heart's-ease no more the wandering shepherds found ;
    No more the nymphs its snowy form possess ;
Its white now changed to purple by Love's wound,
    Heart's-ease no more,—'tis Love-in-idleness.

                    MRS. BRINSLEY SHERIDAN.

THE ALPINE VIOLET.

THE spring is come, the Violet's gone,
The first-born child of the early sun;
With us she is but a winter flower,
The snow on the hills cannot blast her bower;
And she lifts up her dewy eye of blue,
To the youngest sky of the self-same hue;

But when the spring comes with her host
Of flowers, that flower, beloved the most,
Shrinks from the crowd, that may confuse
Her heavenly odours and virgin hues.

Pluck the others, but still remember
Their herald, out of dim December;
The morning star of all the flowers,
The pledge of day-light's lengthened hours;
And, 'mid the roses, ne'er forget,
The virgin, virgin Violet.

BYRON.

LE VIOLE,

Belle, fresche, e purpure Viole,
　　Che quella candidissima man colse,
　　Qual pioggia, o qual pure aer produr volse,
Tanto più vaghi fior che far non suole?
Qual rugiada qual terra, over qual sole
　　Tante vaghe bellezze in voi raccolse?
　　Onde il soave odor Natura tolse,
O il ciel che ha tanto ben degnar ne vuole?

LORENZO DE MEDICI.

THE VIOLET AND THE PANSY.

Far from his hive, one summer's day,
　　A young and yet unpractised bee,
Borne on his tender wings away,
　　Went forth the flowery world to see.

The morn, the noon, in play he passed;
　　But when the shades of evening came,
No parent brought the due repast,
　　And faintness seized his little frame.

By nature urged, by instinct led,
   The bosom of a flower he sought,
Where streams mourned round a mossy bed,
   And Violets all the bank enwrought.

Of kindred race, but brighter dyes,
   On that fair bank a Pansy grew,
That borrowed from indulgent skies,
   A violet shade, a purple hue.

The tints that streamed with glossy gold,
   The violet shade, the purple hue,
The stranger wondered to behold ;
   And to its beauteous bosom flew.

In vain he seeks some virtues there,
   No soul-sustaining charms abound,
No honeyed sweetness to repair
   The languid waste of life is found.

An aged bee, whose labours led
   To these fair springs and meads of gold,
His feeble wing, his drooping head
   Beheld, and pitied to behold.

" Fly, fond adventurer ! fly the art
   That courts thine eye with fond attire ;
Who smiles to win the heedless heart,
   Will smile to see that heart expire.

" This modest flower, of humble view,
   That boasts no depth of glowing dyes,
Arrayed in unbespangled blue,
   The simple clothing of the skies;

" This flower with balmy sweetness blest,
   May yet thy languid life renew :"
He said, and to the Violet's breast
   The little wanderer faintly flew.

                                   LANGHORNE.

THE VIOLET.

The Violet in her greenwood bower,
   Where birchen boughs with hazels mingle,
May boast herself the fairest flower,
   In glen, or copse, or forest dingle.

Though fair her gems of azure hue,
   Beneath the dew-drop's weight reclining,
I've seen an eye of lovelier blue,
   More sweet through watery lustre shining.

The summer sun that dew shall dry,
   Ere yet the day be past its morrow;—
Nor longer in my false love's eye
   Remained the tear of parting sorrow.

                                   SIR. W. SCOTT.

PANSY VIOLET.

(Heartsease, or Love-in-idleness.)

THAT very time I saw (but thou couldst not),
Flying between the cold moon and the earth,
Cupid all armed : a certain aim he took
At a fair vestal, throned by the west ;
And loosed his love-shaft smartly from his bow,
As it should pierce a hundred thousand hearts.
But I might see young Cupid's fiery shaft
Quencht in the chaste beams of the watery moon ;
And the imperial votaress passed on,
In maiden meditation, fancy-free * :
Yet marked I where the bolt of Cupid fell ;
It fell upon a little western flower,
Before milk-white, now purple with love's wound ;
And maidens call it Love-in-idleness.

MIDSUMMER NIGHT'S DREAM.

* This was intended by Shakspeare as a compliment to
our maiden queen, Elizabeth.

THE VIOLET.

(Viola odorata.)

Sweet lowly plant! once more I bend
  To hail thy presence here,
Like a beloved returning friend,
  From absence doubly dear.

Wert thou for ever in our sight,
  Might we not love thee less?
But *now* thou bringest new delight,
  Thou *still* hast power to bless.

Still doth thine April presence bring
  Of April joys a dream;
When life was in its sunny spring—
  A fair unrippled stream.

And still thine exquisite perfume,
  Is precious as of old;
And still thy modest tender bloom,
  It joys me to behold.

It joys and cheers, whone'er I see
  Pain on earth's meek ones press,
To think the storm that rends the tree,
  Scathes not thy lowliness.

And thus may human weakness find,
    E'en in thy lowly flower,
An image cheering to the mind,
    In many a trying hour.

M.

Belfast.   *From " Flowers of all Hue."*

VIOLETS.

A SONNET.

BEAUTIFUL are you in your lowliness;
    Bright in your hues, delicious in your scent,
    Lovely your modest blossoms downward bent,
As shrinking from our gaze, yet prompt to bless
The passer-by with fragrance, and express
    How gracefully, though mutely, eloquent
    Are unobtrusive worth, and meek content,
Rejoicing in their own obscure recess.
Delightful flowerets! at the voice of Spring,
    Your buds unfolded to its sunbeams bright;
    And though your blossoms soon shall fade from sight,
Above your lowly birth-place birds shall sing,
And from your clust'ring leaves the glow-worm fling
    The emerald glory of its earth-born light.

B. BARTON.— *Poetic Vigils.*

THE WALL-FLOWER.

This is a native of Britain, but now found wild in France, Spain, and Switzerland. It is a very hardy plant, bearing our severest winters, particularly on old walls and ruins, where it becomes much stronger and more woody than in the ground. Its fragrance is so well known and admired, that we find it in the gardens of both rich and poor. A small bunch of the flowers is sufficient to scent a large room.

Were it scarce and more difficult to raise, we should prize it as one of our choicest flowers; for it not only refreshes us with its bright green leaves all the winter, but from an early period in the spring, until late in the autumn, we are regaled with the fragrance of its flowers, and with its gay appearance in the parterre. The colours are sometimes exceedingly rich, varying from a warm yellow to a rich brown or deep red corolla, that vies with velvet in richness. So great a favourite is this plant with writers of romance, both in prose and verse, that we generally find it embellish all romantic castles and ruins.

Class, TETRADYNAMIA.   *Order*, SILIQUOSA.

W.

M. Spratt. del

THE WALL-FLOWER.

To me thy site disconsolate,
  On turret, wall, or tower,
Makes thee appear misfortune's mate,
  And desolation's dower.

Thou ask'st no kindly cultured soil
  Thy native bed to be ;
Thou need'st not man's officious toil
  To plant or water thee.

Sown by the winds, thou meekly rear'st
  On ruins' crumbling crest,
Thy fragile form ; and there appear'st
  In smiling beauty drest.

There in the bleak and earthless bed,
  Thou brav'st the tempest's strife ;
And giv'st what else were cold and dead,
  A lingering glow of life.

                              BARTON.

M

TO THE WALL-FLOWER.

I WILL not praise the often-flattered rose,
  Or virgin-like, with blushing charms half seen,
Or when in dazzling splendour, like a queen,
  All her magnificence of state she shows;
No, nor that nun-like lily, which but blows
  Beneath the valley's cool and shady screen;
Nor yet the sunflower, that with warrior mien,
  Still eyes the orb of glory where it glows;
But thou, neglected Wall-flower, to my breast
  And muse art dearest, wildest, sweetest flower,
To whom alone the privilege is given
  Proudly to root thyself above the rest,
As genius does, and from the rocky tower
  Send fragrance to the purest breath of heaven.

ANON.

THE WALL-FLOWER.

FROM THE FABLES OF FLORA.

" WHY loves my flower, the sweetest flower,
  That swells the golden breast of May,
Thrown rudely o'er yon ruined tower,
  To waste her solitary day ?

" Why, when the mead, the spicy vale,
  The grove and genial garden call,
Will she her fragrant soul exhale,
  Unheeded on the lonely wall !

" For never sure was beauty born
  To live in death's deserted shade !
Come, lovely flower, my banks adorn,
  My banks for life and beauty made."

Thus pity waked the tender thought,
  And by her sweet persuasion led,
To seize the hermit flower I sought,
  And bear her from her stony bed.

I sought—but sudden on mine ear
   A voice in hollow murmurs broke,
And smote my heart with holy fear,
   The Genius of the Ruin spoke.

" From thee be far th' ungentle deed,
   The honours of the dead to spoil,
Or take the sole remaining meed,
   The flower that crowns their former toil!

" Nor deem that flower the garden's foe,
   Or fond to grace this barren shade;
'Tis nature tells her to bestow
   Her honours on the lonely dead.

" For this, obedient zephyrs bear
   Her light seeds round yon turret's mould,
And undispersed by tempests there,
   They rise in vegetable gold.

" Nor shall thy wonder wake to see
   Such desert scenes distinction crave;
Oft have they been, and oft shall be
   Truth's, Honour's, Valour's, Beauty's, grave.

" Where longs to fall that rifted spire,
   As weary of the insulting air;
The poet's thought, the warrior's fire,
   The lover's sighs are sleeping there.

" When that too shakes the trembling ground,
　　Borne down by some tempestuous sky,
And many a slumbering cottage round
　　Startles.—how still their hearts will lie !

" Of them who, wrapt in earth so cold,
　　No more the smiling day shall view ;
Should many a tender tale be told,
　　For many a tender thought is due.

" Hast thou not seen some lover pale,
　　When evening brought the pensive hour,
Step slowly o'er the shadowy vale,
　　And stop to pluck the frequent flower ?

" Those flowers he surely meant to strew
　　On lost affection's lowly cell,
Though there, as fond remembrance grew,
　　Forgotten from his hand they fell.

" Has not for thee, the fragrant thorn
　　Been taught her first rose to resign ?
With vain but pious fondness borne
　　To deck thy Nancy's honoured shrine ?

" 'Tis nature pleading in the breast,
　　Fair memory of her works to find ;
And when to fate she yields the rest,
　　She claims the monumental mind.

" Why, else, the o'ergrown paths of time
   Would thus the lettered sage explore ;
With pain these crumbling ruins climb
   And on the doubtful sculpture pore ?

" Why seeks he, with unwearied toil,
   Through death's dim walk to urge his way ;
Reclaim his long-asserted spoil,
   And lead oblivion into day ?

" 'Tis nature prompts, by toil or fear
   Unmoved, to range through death's domain ;
The tender parent loves to hear
   Her children's story told again.

" Treat not with scorn his thoughtful hours,
   If haply near these haunts he stray ;
Nor take the fair enliv'ning flowers
   That bloom to cheer his lonely way."

                LANGHORNE.

THE WALL-FLOWER.

The wall-flower—the wall-flower!
  How beautiful it blooms!
It gleams above the ruin'd tower,
  Like sunlight over tombs;
It sheds a halo of repose
  Around the wrecks of time;—
To beauty give the flaunting rose,
  The wall-flower is sublime.

Flower of the solitary place!
  Grey Ruin's golden crown!
That lendest melancholy grace
  To haunts of old renown;
Thou mantlest o'er the battlement,
  By strife or storm decayed;
And fillest up each envious rent
  Time's canker-tooth hath made.

Whither hath fled the choral band
  That fill'd the abbey's nave?

Yon dark sepulchral yew-trees stand
   O'er many a level grave ;
In the belfry's crevices, the dove
   Her young brood nurseth well,
Whilst thou, lone flower ! dost shed above
   A sweet decaying smell.

In the season of the tulip cup,
   When blossoms clothe the trees,
How sweet to throw the lattice up,
   And scent thee on the breeze.
The butterfly is then abroad,
   The bee is on the wing,
And on the hawthorn by the road
   The linnets sit and sing.

Sweet wall-flower – sweet wall-flower !
   Thou conjurest up to me,
Full many a soft and sunny hour
   Of boyhood's thoughtless glee ;
When joy from out the daisies grew,
   In woodland pastures green,
And summer skies were far more blue
   Than since they e'er have been.

Now autumn's pensive voice is heard
   Amid the yellow bowers,
The robin is the regal bird,
   And thou the Queen of Flowers !

He sings on the laburnum trees,
  Amid the twilight dim,
And Araby ne'er gave the breeze
  Such scents as thou to him.

Rich is the pink, the lily gay,
  The rose is summer's guest;
Bland are thy charms when these decay—
  Of flowers, first, last, and best!
There may be gaudier on the bower,
  And statelier on the tree;
But, wall-flower, loved wall-flower;
  Thou art the flower for me!

                    DAVID MACBETH MOIR.

THE WALL-FLOWER.

AND well the lonely infant knew
Recesses where the Wall-flower grew,
And honey-suckle loved to crawl
Up the low crag and ruin'd wall;
I deem'd such nooks the sweetest shade,
The sun in all his round survey'd,
And still I thought that shattered tower,
The mightiest work of human power.

                    WALTER SCOTT.

YELLOW WATER-FLAG.

(*Iris pseud-Acorus.*)

Tuis plant is common in marshes, and on the borders of rivers; and adds much to the beauty of their appearance, by its showy yellow flowers, which appear in the beginning of July.

This bright Lily of the wave, so pleasing to the eye, is devoid of perfume, unlike the Iris Florentina, which is one of the most delicate perfumes we have. The root of the Yellow Water-Flag, or Iris, is sometimes used instead of galls in the making of ink.

" Amid its waving swords, in flaming gold, the *Iris* towers."

Class, TRIANDRIA. Order, MONOGYNIA.

Y.

WATER-LILIES.

Come away, elves! while the dew is sweet,
Come to the dingles where fairies meet;
Know that the Lilies have spread their bells,
O'er all the pools in our forest dells;
Stilly and lightly their vases rest
On the quivering sleep of the water's breast,
Catching the sunshine thro' leaves that throw
To their scented bosoms an emerald glow;
And a star from the depth of each pearly cup,
A golden star unto heaven looks up,
As if seeking its kindred, where bright they lie,
Set in the blue of the summer sky.
Come away! under arching boughs we'll float,
Making those urns each a fairy boat;
We'll row them with reeds o'er the fountains free,
And a tall flag-leaf shall our streamer be;
And we'll send out wild music so sweet and low,
It shall seem from the bright flower's heart to flow,
As if 'twere a breeze with a flute's low sigh,
Or water-drops trained into melody.
Come away! for the Midsummer sun grows strong,
And the life of the Lily may not be long.

MRS. HEMANS' NATIONAL LYRICS.

YELLOW-FLAG, OR THE WATER-LILY.

———— How peaceful sails
Yon little fleet, the wild duck and her brood.
Fearless of harm, they row their easy way;
The Water-Lily, 'neath the plumy prows,
Dips, reappearing in their dimpled track.

GRAHAME.

THOSE groups of lovely date-trees bending,
    Languidly their leaf-crowned heads,
Like youthful maids, when sleep descending
    Warns them to their silken beds;—
Those virgin Lilies, all the night
    Bathing their beauties in the lake,
That they may rise more fresh and bright,
    When their beloved sun's awake.

MOORE.

THE WATER-LILIES;

OR,

A VOYAGER'S DREAM OF LAND.

THERE's a spring in the woods by my sunny home,
Afar from the dark sea's tossing foam;
Oh! the fall of that fountain is sweet to hear,
As a song from the shore to the sailor's ear!
And the sparkle which up to the sun it throws,
Through the feathery fern and the olive boughs,
And the gleam on its path as it steals away
Into deeper shades from the sultry day;
And the large Water-Lilies that o'er its bed,
Their pearly leaves to the soft light spread;
These haunt me! I dream of that bright spring's flow,
I thirst for its rills like a wounded roe.

MRS. HEMANS.

N

CUPID'S BARK.

He little knew how well the boy
   Can float upon a goblet's stream,
Lighting them with his smile of joy;—
   As bards have seen him in their dreams,
Down the blue Ganges floating glide,
   Upon a rosy Lotus wreath *,
Catching new lustre from the tide,
   That with his image shone beneath.

MOORE.

* The Indians feign that Cupid was first seen floating
down the Ganges on the Nymphæa Netumbo.

Z.

ZEDOARY.

(*Zedoary.*)

THIS plant is a native of the East Indies, and but little known in this country, although it would grace the greenhouse from the beauty of its blossom. The roots are imported into England for medicinal purposes; but of late years have gone much out of use: they have an agreeable camphoraceous smell, and a bitter aromatic taste.

Class, MONANDRIA.   *Order*, MONOGYNIA.

ZEDOARY.

OFFSPRING of India, decked with beauteous flower,
How oft I've watched thee in my orange grove,
At morning's dawn and at the evening hour,
With wonder viewed, and praised the Pow'r above.
From earliest years I loved thee more, dear flower,
Than all the florist's endless arts could raise ;
A parent planted thee to deck her favourite bower :
No more her love, no more her lips shall praise
Your flowers *, nor her I ever more shall see ;
But memory sad recals the past to me.

* A young lady having brought a favourite plant from India; but which died on her reaching England.

FLORA AND THALIA.

—

MISCELLANEOUS POEMS.

THERE IS RELIGION IN A FLOWER;
ITS STILL SMALL VOICE IS AS THE VOICE OF CONSCIENCE:
MOUNTAINS AND OCEANS, PLANETS, SUNS, AND SYSTEMS,
BEAR NOT THE IMPRESS OF ALMIGHTY POWER
IN CHARACTERS MORE LEGIBLE THAN THOSE
WHICH HE HAS WRITTEN ON THE TINIEST FLOWER,
WHOSE LIGHT BELL BENDS BENEATH THE DEW-DROP'S WEIGHT.

HENRY G. BELL.

MISCELLANEOUS POEMS.

TO A MOUNTAIN DAISY.

ON TURNING ONE DOWN WITH THE PLOUGH.

Wee, modest, crimson-tipped flow'r,
Thou'st met me in an evil hour ;
For I maun crush amang the stoure
        Thy slender stem ;
To spare thee now is past my pow'r,
        Thou bonnie gem.

Alas ! it's no thy neebor sweet,
The bonnie lark, companion meet !
Bending thee 'mang the dewy weet !
        Wi' spreckled breast,
When upward-springing, blythe to greet
        The purpling east.

Cauld blew the bitter-biting north
Upon thy early, humble birth;
Yet cheerfully thou glinted forth
   Amid the storm,
Scarce rear'd above the parent earth
   Thy tender form.

The flaunting flow'rs our gardens yield,
High shelt'ring woods and wa's maun shield;
But thou, beneath the random bield
   O' clod or stane,
Adorns the histie stibble-field,
   Unseen, alane.

There in thy scanty mantle clad,
Thy snawy bosom sunward spread,
Thou lifts thy unassuming head
   In humble guise;
But now the share up-tears thy bed,
   And low thou lies!

Such is the fate of artless maid,
Sweet flow'ret of the rural shade!
By love's simplicity betray'd,
   And guileless trust;
Till she, like thee, all soil'd is laid
   Low i' the dust.

Such is the fate of simple Bard,
On life's rough ocean luckless starr'd !
Unskilful he to note the card
          Of prudent lore,
Till billows rage, and gales blow hard,
            And whelm him o'er!

Such fate to suff'ring worth is giv'n,
Who long with wants and woes has striv'n,
By human pride or cunning driv'n
          To mis'ry's brink,
Till wrench'd of ev'ry stay but Heav'n,
           He, ruin'd, sink !

Ev'n thou who mourn'st the Daisy's fate,
That fate is thine—no distant date ;
Stern ruin's ploughshare drives, elate,
          Full on thy bloom,
Till crush'd beneath the furrow's weight,
           Shall be thy doom!
                        BURNS.

BANKS OF DEVON.

How pleasant the banks of the clear-winding Devon,
With green-spreading bushes, and flowers blooming fair ;
But the Bonniest flower on the banks of the Devon,
Was once a sweet bud on the braes of the Ayr.

Mild be the sun on this sweet-blushing flower,
In the gay rosy morn, as it bathes in the dew !
And gentle the fall of the soft vernal shower,
That steals on the evening each leaf to renew.

O, spare the dear blossom, ye orient breezes,
With chill hoary wing as ye usher the dawn !
And far be thou distant, thou reptile that seizes
The verdure and pride of the garden and lawn !

Let Bourbon exult in his gay gilded lilies,
And England, triumphant, display her proud rose ;
A fairer than either adorns the green valleys,
Where Devon, sweet Devon, meandering flows.

BURNS.

VERS A MADAME DE CH * * *.

SUR SES TABLEAUX DES FLEURS.

J'ENJOUIS de ces fleurs si belles;
   J' admire ce pinçeau divin,
Et ces roses si naturelles,
   Que le papillon incertain
Viendra voltiger autour d'elles,
   L'abeille y chercher son butin,
Les fleurs ne brillent qu'un matin;
   Les votres sont immortelles.
   Ah! si j'avois votre talent,
Je peindrais un objêt charmant,
   Paré dès graces du jeune âge,
Qui plait dès le premier instant,
   Et chaque instant plait d'avantage;
Dans l'amitié tendre et constant,
Sincère sans être imprudent,
   Naïf et fin, sensible et sage.
Aisément on devineroit
   Quel auroit été mon modèle;
Ch * * * seule ignoreroit,
   Que le portrait est d'après elle.

M: DE ST. LAMBERT.

FADING FLOWERS.

The morning flowers display their sweets,
 And gay their silken leaves unfold,
As careless of the noontide heats,
 As fearless of the evening cold.

Nipt by the wind's untimely blast,
 Parch'd by the sun's directer ray,
The momentary glories waste,
 The short-liv'd beauties die away.

So blooms the human face divine,
 When youth its pride of beauty shows;
Fairer than spring the colours shine,
 And sweeter than the virgin rose.

But worn by slowly rolling years,
 Or broke by sickness in a day,
The fading glory disappears,
 The short-lived beauties die away.

Yet these new-rising from the tomb,
 With lustre brighter far shall shine,
Revive with ever-during bloom,
 Safe from diseases and decline.

Let sickness blast, let death devour,
   If heaven but recompense our pains;
Perish the grass and fade the flower,
   If firm the word of God remains!

                        C. WESLEY.

A MOTHER'S DIRGE OVER HER CHILD.

BRING me flowers all young and sweet,
That I may strew the winding sheet,
Where calm thou sleepest, baby fair,
With roseless cheek and auburn hair!

Bring me the rosemary, whose breath
Perfumed the wild and desert heath;
The lily of the vale, which, too,
In silence and in beauty grew.

Bring cypress from some sunless spot,
Bring me the blue forget-me-not;
That I may strew them o'er thy bier,
With long-drawn sigh and gushing tear.

Oh, what upon this earth doth prove
So steadfast as a mother's love!
Oh, what on earth can bring relief,
Or solace to a mother's grief!

             o

No more, my baby, shalt thou lie,
With drowsy smile and half-shut eye,
Pillowed upon my fostering breast
Serenely sinking into rest!

The grave must be thy cradle, now;
The wild-flowers o'er thy breast shall grow,
While still my heart, all full of thee,
In widowed solitude shall be.

No taint of earth, no thought of sin,
E'er dwelt thy stainless breast within,
And God hath laid thee down to sleep,
Like a pure pearl below the deep.

Yea! from mine arms thy soul hath flown
Above, and found the heavenly throne,
To join that blest angelic ring,
That aye around the altar sing.

Methought when years had rolled away,
That thou wouldst be my age's stay;
And often have I dreamt to see
The boy—the youth—the man in thee!

But thou hast past! for ever gone,
To leave me childless and alone,
Like Rachel pouring tear on tear,
And looking not for comfort here!

Farewell, my child, the dews shall fall,
At noon and evening, o'er thy pall:
And daisies, when the vernal year
Revives, upon thy turf appear.

The earliest snow-drop there shall spring,
And lark delight to fold his wing;
And roses pale, and lilies fair,
With perfume load the summer air!

Adieu, my babe! if life were long,
This would be even a heavier song;
But years, like phantoms, quickly pass,
They look to us from memory's glass.

Soon on death's couch shall I recline;
Soon shall my head be laid with thine;
And sundered spirits meet above,
To live for evermore in love.

MOIR.

The twining jasmine and the blushing rose,
With lavish grace their morning scents disclose;
The smelling tuberose and jonquil declare
The stronger impulse of an ev'ning air.

PRIOR.

o 2

TO ———.

I send the Lilies given to me;
  Though long before thy hand they touch,
I know that they must withered be;
  But yet reject them not as such:
For I have cherished them as dear,
  Because they yet may meet thine eye,
And guide thy soul to mine, even here,
  When thou behold'st them drooping nigh,
And know'st them gathered by the Rhine,
And offered from my heart to thine!

The river nobly foams and flows,
  The charm of this enchanted ground,
And all its thousand turns disclose,
  Some fresher beauty varying round;
The haughtiest breast its wish might bound,
  Through life to dwell delighted here;
Nor could on earth a spot be found,
  To Nature and to me so dear,
Could thy dear eyes, in following mine,
Still sweeten more these banks of Rhine!

                          ' BYRON.

THE NOSEGAY.

I CULLED for my love a fresh nosegay, one day;
  She smiled as I flew to her side;
I checked the soft sunbeam of pleasure's bright ray,
  While thus I, half playfully, cried :—
" Those lilies and sweets, gentle maid, are like yours,
  This nosegay thy excellence tells;
The rose to the eye, like thy beauty, allures,
  But its thorn, like thy virtue, repels."

The jasmine, so simple, so sweet to the sense,
  Of gentle and delicate hue,
Recals all thy talents, so void of pretence,
  So modest, yet exquisite too;
The woodbine, where bees love their treasures to seek
  Is a type of affection like mine;
And oh ! may this innocent flow'r my wish speak,
  And heartsease for ever be thine !

                                        SONG.

AUX FLEURS.

FLEURS charmantes ! par vous la nature est plus belle,
Dans ses brillants travaux l'art vous prend pour
        modèle ;
Simples tributs du cœur, vos dons sont chaque jour
Offerts par l'amitié, hazardés par l'amour.

D'embellir la beauté vous obtenez la gloire ;
Le laurier vous permet de parer la victoire ;
Plus d'un hameau vous donne en prix à la pudeur ;
L'autel même où de Dieu repose la grandeur,
Se parfume au printemps de vos douces offrandes,
Et la Religion sourit à vos guirlandes.
Mais c'est dans nos jardins qu'est votre heureux sejour.
Filles de la rosée et de l'astre du jour,
Venez donc ; de nos champs decorer le theâtre.

   *   *   *   *   *

Sans obéir aux lois d'un art capricieux
Fleurs, parure des champs et délices des yeux,
De vos riches couleurs venez peindre la terre.
Venez ; mais n'allez pas dans les buis d'un parterre,
Renfermer vos appas tristement relégués ;
Que vos heureux trésors soient partout prodigués,
Tantôt de ces tapis émaillez la verdure ;
Tantôt de ces sentiers egayez la bordure ;
Serpentez en guirlande ; entourez ces berceaux,
En méandres brillants, courez au bord des eaux,
Ou tapissez ces mûrs, ou dans cette corbeille
Du choix de vos parfums embarrassez l'abeille.

DE DELILLE. " *Les Jardins.*"

TO AN EARLY PRIMROSE.

MILD offspring of a dark and sullen sire!
Whose modest form, so delicately fine,
  Was nursed in whirling storms,
  And cradled in the winds.

Thee, when young Spring first questioned Winter's sway,
And dared the sturdy blusterer to the fight,
  Thee on this bank he threw,
  To mark his victory.

In the low vale, the promise of the year,
Serene, thou openest to the nipping gale,
  Unnoticed and alone,
  Thy tender elegance.

So Virtue blooms, brought forth amid the storms
Of chill adversity; in some lone walk
  Of life she rears her head,
  Obscure and unobserved;

While every bleaching breeze that on her blows,
Chastens her spotless purity of breast,
  And hardens her to bear
  Serene the ills of life.

        KIRKE WHITE.

THE BUD OF THE ROSE.

HER mouth, which a smile,
Devoid of all guile,
Half opened to view,
Is the bud of the rose,
In the morning that blows,
Impearled with the dew.
More fragrant her breath
Than the flow'r-scented heath
At the dawning of day;
The lily's perfume,
The hawthorn in bloom,
Or the blossoms of May.

OLD SONG.

MORTE DI DARDINELLO.

COME purpureo fior languendo muore,
Che'l vomere al passar tagliato lassa,
O come carco di superchio umore
Il Papaver nell'orto il capo abbassa;
Così giù della faccia ognio colore,
Cadendo, Dardinel, di vita passa:
Passa di vita, e fa passar con lui
L'ardire e la virtù du tutti i sui.

ARIOSTO.   *Orlando.*

THE SUNFLOWER.

Who can unpitying see the flow'ry race
Shed by the moon their new flush'd bloom resign
Before the parching beam? so fades the face,
When fevers revel through their azure veins,
But one the lofty follower of the sun,
Sad when he sets, shuts up her yellow leaves,
Drooping all night, and when he warm returns
Points her enamour'd bosom to his ray.

THOMSON.

THE SNOWDROP.

Already now the snowdrop dares appear,
The first pale blossom of th' unripen'd year;
As Flora's breath, by some transforming power,
Had chang'd an icicle into a flower,
Its name and hue the scentless plant retains,
And winter lingers in its icy veins.

BARBAULD.

A CHRISTMAS WREATH.

A WREATH for merry Christmas quickly twine,
A wreath for the bright red sparkling wine,
    Though roses are dead
    And their bloom is fled,
Yet for Christmas a bonnie, bonnie wreath we'll twine.
Away to the wood where the bright holly grows,
And its red berries blush amid winter snows,
Away to the ruin where the green ivy clings,
And around the dark fane its verdure flings;
  Hey! for the ivy and holly so bright,
  They are the garlands for Christmas night.

LOUISA ANNE TWAMLEY.

A DAISY'S OFFERING.

THINK of the flowers culled for thee,
  In vest of silvery white,
When other flowers perchance you see,
  Not fairer, but more bright.

Sweet roses and carnations gay,
  Have but a summer's reign;
I mingle with the buds of May,
  Join drear December's train.

A simple unassuming flower,
  'Mid showers and storms I bloom;
I'll decorate thy lady's bower,
  And blossom on thy tomb.

FIELD FLOWERS.

Ye field flowers! the gardens eclipse you, 'tis true,
Yet, wildlings of nature, I dote upon you;
    For ye waft me to summers of old,
When the earth teemed around me with fairy delight,
And when daisies and buttercups gladdened my sight,
    Like treasures of silver and gold.

I love you for lulling me back into dreams,
Of the blue Highland mountains and echoing streams,
    And of broken blades breathing their balm;
While the deer was seen glancing in sunshine remote,
And the deep mellow crush of the wood-pigeon's note
    Made music that sweetened the calm.

Not a pastoral song has a pleasanter tune
Than ye speak to my heart, little wildlings of June;
    Of old ruinous castles ye tell;
I thought it delightful your beauties to find,
When the magic of Nature first breathed on my mind,
    And your blossoms were part of her spell.

E'en now what affections the violet awakes ;
What loved little islands, twice seen in their lakes,
    Can the wild water-lily restore.
What landscapes I read in the primrose's looks;
What pictures of pebbles and minnowy brooks
    In the vetches that tangle the shore.

Earth's cultureless buds! to my heart ye were dear
Ere the fever of passion, or ague of fear,
    Had scathed my existence's bloom ;
Once I welcome you more, in life's passionless stage,
With the visions of youth to revisit my age,
    And I wish you to grow on my tomb.

CAMPBELL.

THE PURPOSE OF FLOWERS.

BEAUTIFUL flowers, whose tender forms
    Survive the deadly lightning's glare,
And bend your bosoms to the storms
    That ride upon the midnight air !

Say, were ye only born to fade;
    Or were your tints and odours given,
To give the spirit in the shade
    Of this dull world some glimpse of heaven?

W. MARTIN.

LA FARFALLA SULLA ROSA.

Farfalletta dorata
Sulla Rosa sedea,
E superba dicea
Per me la Rosa è nata,
E spiegava le alette
E le fresche cimette
Del fior giova scotendo;
E scherzando e giojendo
Repetea baldanjosa
Nata è per me la Rosa.
On mentre qual reina
Sta su quel trono e parla,
Giovine contadina
S'invoglia di predarla:
La man furtiva stende
Entro il pugno la prende
Le pinte ali le toglie
E poi la Rosa coglie,
" Non ti fidar se infiora
Tuoi dì sorte pomposa;
Pensa che sei tu ancora
Farfalla sulla Rosa."

BERTOLA.

P

THE DIAL OF FLOWERS*.

'Twas a lovely thought to mark the hours,
  As they floated in light away,
By the opening and the folding flowers,
  That laugh to the summer's day.

Thus had each moment its own rich hue,
  And its graceful cup and bell,
In whose coloured vase might sleep the dew,
  Like a pearl in an ocean shell.

To such sweet signs might the time have flowed
  In a golden current on,
Ere from the garden, man's first abode,
  The glorious guests were gone.

So might the days have been brightly told—
  Those days of song and dreams—
When shepherds gathered their flocks of old,
  By the blue Arcadian streams.

  * This dial is said to have been formed by Linnæus.
It marked the hours by the opening and closing, at regular
intervals, of the flowers arranged in it.

So in those isles of delight, that rest
   Far off in a breezeless main,
Which many a bark, with a weary guest,
   Has sought, but still in vain.

Yet is not life, in its real flight,
   Marked thus—even thus—on earth,
By the closing of one hope's delight,
   And another's gentle birth?

Oh ! let us live so, that flower by flower,
   Shutting in turn, may leave
A lingerer still, for the sun-set hour,
   A charm for the shaded eve.

                MRS. HEMANS.

COWSLIP AND ROSE.

THE cowslip smiles in brighter yellow drest,
Than that which veils the nubile virgin's breast ;
A fairer red stands blushing in the rose,
Than that which on the bridegroom's vestments flows.

                PRIOR.

THE DAISY IN INDIA.

Dr. Carey having deposited, in his garden at
Serampore, the earth in which a number of English
seeds had been conveyed to him from his native land,
was agreeably surprised by the appearance, in due
time, of this " wee, modest, crimson-tipped flower."
This circumstance, being stated by the Doctor in a
letter to a friend, suggested the following lines :—

Thrice welcome! little English flower!
    My mother country's, white and red,
In rose or lily, to this hour,
    Never to me such beauty spread—
Transplanted from thine island-bed,
    A treasure in a grain of earth;
Strange as a spirit from the dead,
    Thine embryo sprang to birth.

Thrice welcome! little English flower!
    Whose tribes, beneath our natal skies,
Shut close their leaves while vapours lower;
    But when the sun's gay beams arise,
With unabashed but modest eyes,
    Follow his motions to the west,
Nor cease to gaze till day-light dies;
    Then fold themselves to rest.

Thrice welcome! little English flower!
   To this resplendent hemisphere,
Where Flora's giant offspring tower
   In gorgeous liveries all the year,
Thou, only thou art little here,
   Like worth unfriended and unknown,
Yet to my British heart more dear
   Than all the torrid zone.

Thrice welcome! little English flower!
   Of early scenes, beloved by me,
While happy in my father's bower,
   Thou shalt the bright memorial be!
Thy fairy sports of infancy,
   Youth's golden age, and manhood's prime,
Home, country, kindred, friends—with thee,
   Are mine in this far clime.

Thrice welcome! little English flower!
   I'll rear thee with a trembling hand:
O for the April sun and shower,
   The sweet May dews of that fair land,
Where Daisies, thick as star-light, stand
   In every walk!—that here might shoot
Thy scions, and thy buds expand
   A hundred from one root.

Thrice welcome! little English flower,
   To me the pledge of hope unseen!
When sorrow would my soul o'erpower
   For joys that were, or might have been,

I'll call to mind how fresh and green,
    I saw thee waking from the dust;
Then turn to Heaven, with brow serene,
    And place in God my trust!

                            J. MONTGOMERY.

THE FLOWERS OF THE FIELD PROVE GOD'S EXISTENCE.

Not worlds on worlds, in phalanx deep,
Need we to prove a God is here;
The Daisy, fresh from Winter's sleep,
Tells of his hand in lines as clear.

For who but He who arched the skies
And pours the day-spring's living flood,
Wond'rous alike in all he tries,
Could raise the Daisy's purple bud?

Mould its green cup, its wiry stem,
Its fringed border nicely spin;
And cut the gold-embossed gem
That, set in silver, gleams within?—

And fling it unrestrained and free,
O'er hill and dale, and desert sod,
That man, where'er he walks, may see
In ev'ry step the stamp of God?

                        DR. MASON GOOD.

A HAPPY COUNTRY DWELLING.

Low was our pretty cot; our tallest rose
Peep'd at the chamber window.   We could hear,
At silent noon, and eve, and early morn,
The sea's faint murmur.   In the open air
Our myrtles blossomed; and across the porch
Thick jasmines twined; the little landscape round
Was green and woody, and refresh'd the eye.
It was a spot which you might aptly call
The Valley of Seclusion!   Once I saw
(Hallowing his sabbath-day by quietness)
A wealthy son of commerce saunter by,
Bristowa's citizen; methought it calm'd
His thirst of idle gold, and made him muse
With wiser feelings; for he paused, and look'd
With a pleased sadness, and he gazed all round,
Then eyed our cottage, and gazed round again,
And sighed, and said it was a blessed place,
And we were blessed.   Oft, with patient ear,
Long listening to the viewless sky-lark's note,
(Viewless, or haply for a moment seen
Gleaming on sunny wing) in whisper'd tones
I've said to my beloved, "Such, sweet girl!
The inobtrusive song of happiness,
Unearthly minstrelsy! then only heard
When the soul seeks to hear, when all is hush'd,
And the heart listens!"

                                        COLERIDGE.

THE CHILD AND FLOWERS.

HAST thou been in the woods with the honey-bee?
Hast thou been with the lamb in the pastures free?
With the hare through the copses and dingles wild?
With the butterfly over the heath, fair child?
Yes; the light fall of thy bounding feet
Hath not startled the wren from her mossy seat;
Yet hast thou rang'd the green forest dells,
And brought back a treasure of buds and bells.

Thou know'st not the sweetness, by antique song,
Breath'd o'er the names of that flow'ry throng:
The woodbine, the primrose, the violet dim,
The lily that gleams by the fountain's brim:
Those are old words, that have made each grove
A dreamy haunt for romance and love;
Each sunny bank, where faint odours lie,
A place for the gushings of poesy.

Thou know'st not the light wherewith fairy lore
Sprinkles the turf and the daisies o'er.
Enough for thee are the dews that sleep,
Like hidden gems in the flower-urns deep;
Enough the rich crimson spots that dwell
'Midst the gold of the cowslip's perfumed cell;
And the scent by the blossoming sweetbriars shed,
And the beauty that bows the wood-hyacinth's head.

Oh! happy child, in thy fawn-like glee,
What is remembrance or thought to thee?
Fill thy bright locks with those gifts of spring;
O'er thy green pathway their colours fling;
Bind them in chaplet and wild festoon—
What if to droop and to perish soon?
Nature hath mines of such wealth—and thou
Never wilt prize its delights as now.

For a day is coming to quell the tone
That rings in thy laughter, thou joyous one!
And to dim thy brow with a touch of care,
Under the gloss of its clustering hair;
And to tame the flash of thy cloudless eyes
Into the stillness of autumn skies;
And to teach thee that grief hath her needful part
'Midst the hidden things of each human heart.

Yet, shall we mourn, gentle child, for this?
Life hath enough of yet holier bliss.
Such be thy portion! the bliss to look
With a reverent spirit through Nature's book;
By fount, by forest, by river's line,
To track the paths of a love divine;
To read its deep meanings—to see and hear
God in earth's garden,—and not to fear.

MRS. HEMANS.

LOVE'S WREATH.

When Love was a child, and went idling round
  Among flowers the whole summer's day,
One morn in the valley a bower he found,
  So sweet it allured him to stay.

O'er head from the trees hung a garland fair,
  A fountain ran darkly beneath ;
'Twas Pleasure that hung the bright flowers up there,
  Love knew it and jumped at the wreath.

But Love did not know, and at his weak years,
  What urchin was likely to know
That sorrow had made of her own salt tears,
  That fountain which murmured below ?

He caught at the wreath but with too much haste,
  As boys when impatient will do,
It fell in those waters of briny taste,
  And the flowers were all wet through.

Yet this is the wreath, he wears night and day ;
  And though it all sunny appears
With Pleasure's own lustre, each leaf, they say,
  Still tastes of the fountain of tears.

MOORE.

TO MAKE A HORTUS SICCUS, OR HERBARIUM.

PERHAPS it may not be unacceptable to our readers to make a few remarks on the benefit of procuring a collection of dried plants: we will therefore quote Sir James Smith's observations on the subject.

"The advantage of preserving specimens of plants, as far as it can be done, for examination at all times and seasons, is abundantly obvious. Notwithstanding the multitude of books filled with descriptions and figures of plants, and however ample such may be, they can teach no more than their authors observed. But when we have the works of nature before us, we can investigate them for ourselves, pursuing any train of inquiry to its utmost extent, nor are we liable to be misled by the errors or misconceptions of others.

"A good practical botanist must be educated among the wild scenes of nature, while a finished theoretical one requires the additional assistance of gardens and books, to which must be superadded the frequent use of a good herbarium. When plants are well dried, the original forms and positions of even their minutest parts, though not their colours, may at any time be restored by immersion in hot water. By this means, the productions of the most distant and various countries, such as no garden could possibly supply, are brought together at once under our eye, at any season of the year. If these be assisted with drawings and descriptions, nothing less than an actual survey of the whole vegetable world in a state of nature could excel such a store of information.

" The greater part of plants dry with facility between the leaves of books, or other paper; the smoother the better.

" If there be plenty of paper, they often dry best without shifting; but if the specimens are crowded they must be taken out frequently, and the paper dried, before they are replaced.

" The great point to be attended to is, that the process should meet with no check. Several vegetables are so tenacious of their vital principle, that they will grow between papers, the consequence of which is a destruction of their proper habit and colour. It is necessary to destroy the life of such, either by immersion in boiling water, or by the application of a hot iron, such as is used for linen, after which they are easily dried.

" I cannot, however, approve of the practice of applying such an iron, as some persons do with great labour and perseverance, till the plants are quite dry, and all their parts incorporated into a smooth flat mass, this renders them unfit for subsequent examination, and destroys their natural habit, the most important thing to be preserved.

" Even in spreading plants between papers, we should refrain from that precise and artificial disposition of their branches, leaves, and other parts, which takes away from their natural aspect, except for the purpose of displaying the internal parts of some one or two of their flowers for ready observation.

" Dried specimens are best preserved by being fastened with weak carpenter's glue to paper, so that they may be turned over without damage. Thick and heavy stalks require the additional support of a few transverse slips of paper, to bind them more firmly down. A half sheet of a convenient size should be allotted to each species.

" One great and mortifying impediment to the perfect preservation of an herbarium, arises from the attacks of insects; to remedy this inconvenience, I have found a solution of corrosive sublimate of mercury in rectified spirits of wine, about two drachms to a pint, with a little camphor, perfectly efficacious, applied with a camel-hair pencil when the specimens are perfectly dry, not before; and if they are not too tender, it is best done before they are pasted, as the spirit extracts a yellow dye from many plants, and stains the paper. A few drops of this solution should be mixed with the glue used for pasting. The herbarium is best kept in a dry room, without a constant fire."

SIR JAMES EDWARD SMITH'S *Introduction to Botany.*

THE MARYGOLD.

When with a serious musing, I behold
The grateful and obsequious marygold,
How duly, every morning, she displays
Her open breast when Phœbus spreads his rays;
How she observes him in his daily walk,
Still bending tow'rds him her small slender stalk;
How, when he down declines, she droops and mourns,
Bedewed as 'twere with tears, till he returns;
And how she veils her flowers when he is gone,
As if she scorned to be looked upon
By an inferior eye; or did contemn
To wait upon a meaner light than him:
When this I meditate, methinks the flowers
Have spirits far more generous than ours,
And give us fair examples to despise,
The servile fawnings and idolatries
Wherewith we court these earthly things below.
Which merit not the service we bestow.
But O, my God! though grovelling I appear
Upon the ground, and have a rooting here
Which hales me downward, yet in my desire
To that which is above me I aspire,
And all my best affections, I profess
To him that is the Sun of Righteousness.
Oh! keep the morning of his incarnation,
The burning noontide of his bitter passion,

The night of his descending, and the height
Of his ascension,—ever in my sight,
That imitating him in what I may,
I never follow an inferior way.

WITHERS.

TO THE CROCUS.

Lowly, sprightly little flower!
　Herald of a brighter bloom,
Bursting in a sunny hour,
　From thy winter tomb.

Hues you bring, bright, gay, and tender,
　As if never to decay;
Fleeting is their varied splendour,—
　Soon, alas! it fades away.

Thus, the hopes I long had cherished,
　Thus, the friends I long had known,
One by one, like you, have perished;
　Blighted—I must fade alone.

R. PATTERSON.

Belfast.

LE LODE DEGLI POMI.

L'ALMA, verde odorata e vaga pianta
Che fu trovata in ciel, che'l pome d'oro
Produsse, onde poi fu l'antica lite
Tra le celesti Dee, c'al terren d'Argo,
Partori mille affanni, e morte a Troia ;
Quella ch'entr'ai giardin lieti e felici
Tra le ninfe d'Esperia in guardia avea
L'omicidial serpente; ond' a Perseo
Fu tanto avaro alfin l'antico Atlante,
Ch'ei divenne del ciel sostegno eterno
Dico il grallo limon, gli Auraci e i cedri,
Ch'entr'ai fini smeraldi, al caldo, al gielo
(Che primavera è loro ovunque saglia,
Ovunque ascenda il sol), pendenti e freschi
Ed acerbi e maturi an sempre i pomi
Ensieme i fior che'l gelsomino e'l giglio
Avanzan di color; l'odore è tale,
Che l'alma Cyterea se n'impie il seno,
Se n'Inghirlanda il Erin.

ALMANNI DEL. COL.

LINES TO A YOUNG LADY,

WITH VERSES ON A VARIETY OF FLOWERS.

SOME lines on many a garden flower,
   And native wildling too, I send;
Trifles like these assume a power
   To please, when offered by a *friend.*

Flowers are the brightest things which earth
   On her broad bosom loves to cherish;
Gay they appear as childhood's mirth,
   Like fading dreams of hope they perish.

In every clime, in every age,
   Mankind have felt their pleasing sway;
And lays to them have decked the page
   Of moralist, and minstrel gay.

By them the lover tells his tale,
   They can his hopes, his fears express;
The maid, when words or looks would fail,
   Can thus a kind return confess.

They wreathe the harp at banquets tried,
   With them we crown the crested brave;
They deck the maid—adorn the bride—
   Or form the chaplets for her grave.

Q 3

If hopes and fervent wishes could
　　Controul futurity's dark veil,
There's not a plant or flower but should
　　Have virtues such as you'd reveal.

You should, like roses, charm the view;
　　Like mignonette, should glad the heart;
Your friends should be like ivy, true,
　　And everlasting where thou art.

As the bright flower, which fables say
　　Turns on its stem, the sun to greet,
Should you, where'er your path might stray,
　　Continued joy and sunshine meet.

But should misfortune dim your road,
　　May you be like that lovely flower,
Which, pressed beneath an adverse load,
　　Breathes secret sweets of balmy power.

And as through sunshine you may go,
　　Or bow beneath affliction's night,
May He who bids the lily grow,
　　Direct and guide your course aright.

R. PATTERSON.

SPRING AND SUMMER FLOWERS.

WHEN every leaf is brightly green,
  When every stem hath sweetest flowers,
And brilliant hues bedeck the scene,
  Throughout the joyous summer hours ;

When sweetest perfumes scent the air,
  When the bright sky hath deepest blue,
When fairest scenes seem doubly fair,
  And all is cloudless to our view ;

Say, with what feelings do we gaze
  Upon the garden's gaudy flowers,
The Rose's tint, the Tulip's blaze,
  The sweet Carnation's spicy powers !

Their beauty greeteth every eye,
  Their perfume floats on every breeze,
Yielding rich incense to the sky,—
  Our love abideth not with these.

But when the Snowdrop's fragile head,
  First timidly attracts our view,
Ere winter's sternest hour hath fled,
  Like friendship to affliction true ;

And when the breath of early spring
   Gives to the modest Primrose birth,
And tempts the Violet to bring
   Her beauty from the sheltering earth;

It is with exquisite delight
   We hail these unassuming flowers,
More dearly precious in our sight,
   Than all that deck our summer bowers.

They are the prized, the cherished few,
   Types of our best affections here;
Our path they beautifully strew,
   And first perchance in gloom appear.

                     M.
            From " Flowers of all Hue."

POETICAL PORTRAIT.

A Violet by a mossy stone,
   Half hidden from the eye,
Fair as a star, when only one
   Is shining in the sky.
               WORDSWORTH.

FLOWERS of the fairest,
   And gems of the rarest,
I find and I gather in country or town;
   But one is still wanting,
   Oh! where is it haunting?
The bud and the jewel must make up my crown.

The Rose with its bright heads,
The diamond that light sheds,
Rich as the sunbeam and pure as the snow;
One gives me its fragrance,
The other its radiance;
But the pearl and the lily where dwell they below?

'Tis years since I knew thee,
But yet should I view thee
With the eye and the heart of my earliest youth;
And feel thy meek beauty,
Add impulse to duty,
The love of the fancy to old ties of truth.

Thou pearl of the deep sea,
That flows in my heart free,
Thou rock-planted lily come hither or send;
'Mid flowers of the fairest,
And gems of the rarest,
I miss thee, I seek thee, my own parted friend!

M. J. JEWSBURY.

LA BRANCHE D'AMANDIER.

DE l'amandier tige fleurie,
Symbole, hélas! de la beauté,
Comme toi, la fleur de la vie,
Fleurit et tombe avant l'été.

Qu'on la néglige ou qu'on la cueille,
   De nos fronts, des mains de l'amour,
Elle s'échappe feuille à feuille,
   Comme nos plaisirs jour à jour.

Savourons ces courtes délices;
   Disputons les mêmes au zephyr;
Épuisons les rians calices,
   De ces parfums qui vont mourir.

Souvent la beauté fugitive
   Ressemble à la fleur du matin,
Qui du front glacé du convive,
   Tombe avant l'heure du festin.

Un jour tombe, un autre se lève;
   Le printemps va s'évanouir;
Chaque fleur que le vent enlève
   Nous dit : Hâtez-vous d'en jouir.

Et puisqu'il faut qu'elles périssent,
   Qu'elles périssent sans retour!
Que les roses ne se flétrissent,
   Que sous les lèvres de l'Amour!

                  DE LAMARTINE.

THE PRIMROSE.

Ask me why I send you here
This sweet infanta of the year?
Ask me why I send to you
This Primrose all bepearled with dew?
I will whisper in your ears,
The sweets of love are washed with tears.

Ask me why this flower does shew,
So yellow-green, and sickly too?
Ask me why the stalk is weak,
And bending, yet it doth not break?
I will answer, these discover,
What fainting hopes are in a lover.

HERRICK.

BRING FLOWERS.

Bring flowers, young flowers, for the festal board,
To wreath the cup ere the wine is poured;
Bring flowers! they are springing in wood and vale,
Their breath floats out on the southern gale;
And the touch of the sunbeam hath waked the rose,
To deck the hall where the bright wine flows.

Bring flowers to strew in the conqueror's path,—
He hath shaken thrones with his stormy wrath!
He comes with the spoils of nations back,
The vines lie crushed in his chariot's track;
The turf looks red where he won the day—
Bring flowers to strew in the conqueror's way.

Bring flowers to the captive's lonely cell,
They have tales of the joyous woods to tell;
Of the free blue streams and the glowing sky,
And the bright world shut from his languid eye:
They will bear him a thought of the sunny hours,
And a dream of his youth,—bring him flowers, wild
    flowers.

Bring flowers, fresh flowers, for the bride to wear!
They were born to blush in her shining hair;
She is leaving the home of her childhood's mirth,
She hath bid farewell to her father's hearth;
Her place is now by another's side—
Bring flowers for the locks of the fair young bride!

Bring flowers, pale flowers, o'er the bier to shed,
A crown for the brow of the early dead!
For this, through its leaves hath the white rose burst,
For this, in the woods was the violet nursed!
Though they smile in vain for what once was ours,
They are love's last gift—bring ye flowers, pale flowers!

Bring flowers to the shrine where we kneel in prayer,
They are Nature's offering, their place is *there !*
They speak of hope to the fainting heart,
With a voice of promise they come and part ;
They sleep in dust through the wintry hours,
They break forth in glory—bring flowers, bright flowers !

MRS. HEMANS.

THE CELANDINE.

Pansies, Lilies, King-cups, Daisies,
Let them live upon their praises ;
   Long as there's a sun that sets,
Primroses will have their glory ;
   Long as there are Violets,
They will have a place in story :
    There's a flower which shall be mine,
    'Tis the little Celandine.

Ere a leaf is on the bush,
In the time before the thrush
   Has a thought about its nest,
Thou wilt come with half a call,
   Spreading out thy glossy breast,
Like a careless prodigal,
    Telling tales about the sun,
    When there's little warmth, or none.

R

Soon as gentle breezes bring
News of winter's vanishing,
    And the children build their bowers,
Sticking 'kerchief plots of mould,
    All about with full-blown flowers,
Thick as sheep in shepherd's fold ; .
    With the proudest thou art there,
    Mantling in the tiny square.

Comfort have thou of thy merit,
Kindly, unassuming spirit !
    Careless of thy neighbourhood,
Thou dost show thy pleasant face
    On the moor and in the wood;
Iu the lane—there's not a place,
    Howsoever mean it be,
    But 'tis good enough for thee.

                              WORDSWORTH.

SUR DES ŒILLETS ARROSÉS PAR LE GRAND CONDÉ.

En voyant ces Œillets, qu'un illustre guerrier
Arrose d'une main qui gagna des batailles ;
Souviens-toi qu'Apollon batissait des murailles,
Et ne t'étonne pas que Mars soit jardinièr.

            MADEMOISELLE DE SCUDERY.

LE MATIN.

Le voile du matin sur les monts se déploie.
Vois, un rayon naissant blanchit la vieille tour,
Et déjà dans les cieux s'unit avec amour,
    Ainsi que la gloire à la joie,
Le premier chant des bois aux premiers feux du jour.

Oui, souris à l'éclat dont le ciel se décore !
Tu verras, si demain le cercueil me dévore,
    Luire à tes yeux en pleurs un soleil aussi beau,
Et les mêmes oiseaux chanter la même aurore,
    Sur mon noir et muët tombeau !

Mais dans l'autre horizon l'âme alors est ravie,
L'avenir sans fin s'ouvre à l'être illimité ;
    Au matin de l'éternité
    On se réveille de la vie,
Comme d'une nuit sombre ou d'un rêve agité.

VICTOR HUGO.

NIGHT-SCENTED FLOWERS.

Call back your odours, lovely flowers,
  From the night-winds, call them back ;
And fold your leaves till the laughing hours
  Come forth in the sunbeam's track.

The lark lies couched in her grassy nest,
  And the honey-bee is gone ;
And all bright things are away to rest,
  Why watch ye here alone ?

" Nay, let our shadowy beauty bloom,
  When the stars give quiet light ;
And let us offer our faint perfume
  On the silent shrine of night.

" Call it not wasted, the scent we lend
  To the breeze, when no step is nigh ;
Oh, thus for ever the earth should send
  Her grateful breath on high !

" And love us as emblems, night's dewy flowers,
  Of hopes unto sorrows given,
That spring through the gloom of the darkest hours
  Looking alone to heaven."

            FROM MRS. HEMANS' NATIONAL LYRICS.

ON PLANTING A TULIP-ROOT.

Here lies a bulb, the child of earth,
  Buried alive beneath the clod,
Ere long to spring, by second birth,
  A new and nobler work of God.

'Tis said that microscopic power
  Might, through his swaddling folds, descry
The infant image of the flower,
  Too exquisite to meet the eye.

This, vernal suns and rains will swell,
  Till from its dark abode it peep,
Like Venus rising from her shell,
  Amidst the spring-tide of the deep.

Two shapely leaves will first unfold;
  Then, on a smooth elastic stem,
The verdant bud shall turn to gold,
  And open in a diadem.

Not one of Flora's brilliant race,
  A form more perfect can display;
Art could not feign more simple grace,
  Nor Nature take a line away.

Yet, rich as morn, of many a hue,
　　When flushing clouds through darkness strike,
The Tulip's petals shine in dew,
　　All beautiful, but none alike.

Kings, on their bridal, might unrobe,
　　To lay their glories at its foot;
And queens their sceptre, crown, and globe,
　　Exchange for blossom, stalk, and root.

Here could I stand and moralise;
　　Lady, I leave that part to thee;
Be thy next birth in Paradise,
　　Thy life to come—eternity.

MONTGOMERY.

THE WREATH*.

Weave a wreath of varied hues,
Here are garlands twining,
For the gay, the brightest choose,
And drooping for the pining.
"LONDON PRIDE," for West-end beaux
Or belles, as fancy ranges;
"HEART'S-EASE" too, in plenty grows,
To meet Dame Fortune's changes.

* See the *Presentation Plate.*

With the Heiress, " MARY-GOLD,"
For men who wish to marry;
" BACHELOR'S BUTTONS " now unfold,
For those who ever tarry.
" LOVE LIES BLEEDING " for the flirt
Its lonely bloom discloses;
Maidens, pray your frowns avert,
Prudes shall wear " PRIMROSES."

In this wreath, for city men
The " STOCK " its blossom raises;
" PINKS " for would-be dandies, then
The simple lack-a " DAISIES;"
Deep " BLUE BELLS " for belles who read,
" JONQUILS " for the scribblers;
" LAUREL " crowns the victor's meed,
And " VIOL-ETS " the fiddler's.

" PASSION-FLOWERS " for lovers' vows,
When they dare confess them;
" ROSES " sweet, for Beauty's brows,
My pray'r is, Heaven bless them.
Lady, may thy pathway be,
Through life, with flowers blended,
" FORGET ME NOT," I ask of thee—
With this, my " Wreath " is ended.

S. J.

ON THE LILY.

——————— BOLD Oxlip, and
The crown imperial ; lilies of all kinds,
The Flower-de-luce being one. Of these I lack
To make you garlands of, and my sweet friend
To strew him o'er and o'er.

WINTER'S TALE.

SHIPWRECKED upon a kingdom where no pity,
No friends, no hope, no kindred, weep for me ;
Almost, no grave allowed me : like the lily,
That once was mistress of the field and flourished,
I'll hang my head and perish.

KING HENRY VIII.

Observe the rising lily's snowy grace,
Observe the various vegetable race ;
They neither toil nor spin, but careless grow,
Yet see how warm they blush ! how bright they glow.
What regal vestments can with them compare ;
What king so shining, or what queen so fair !

PRIOR.

THE BLUE HARE-BELL*.

Have ye ever heard in the twilight dim,
  A low, soft strain,
That ye fancied a distant vesper hymn,
  Borne o'er the plain
By the zephyrs that rise on perfumed wing,
When the sun's last glances are glimmering?

Have ye heard that music, with cadence sweet,
  And merry peal,
Ring out, like the echoes of fairy feet,
  O'er flowers that steal?
And did ye deem that each trembling tone
Was the distant vesper-chime alone?

The source of that whispering strain I'll tell;
  For I've listened oft
To the music faint of the Blue Hare-bell,
  In the gloaming soft;
'Tis the gay fairy-folk the peal who ring,
  At even-time for their banqueting.

---

* These exquisitely beautiful lines have been selected
from a volume, recently published by Mr. Tilt, entitled
"*Poems, with Illustrations*, by Louisa Anne Twamley." A
young lady, who, at the age of *twenty*, is a *Poet*, a *Painter*,
and *her own Engraver*.

And gaily the trembling bells peal out,
   With gentle tongue,
While elves and fairies career about,
   'Mid dance and song.
Oh, roses and lilies are fair to see ;
But the wild Blue-bell is the flower for me.

LOUISA ANNE TWAMLEY.

ON A TIME-PIECE.

WITH A FIGURE OF TIME, PLACED NEAR A VASE OF FLOWERS.

O PAUSE, Old Time, ere o'er my flowers,
   Thy fatal sithe is coldly laid ;
And leave, O leave, some lingering hours,
   Ere Nature's final debt is paid.

Some lingering hours, in which may rise
   The memory of the buried past ;
And I may pour some parting sighs,
   O'er hopes, thoughts, joys, for ever past.

They rise no more—those flowers are shed,
   Whose early fragrance blest my morn ;
They haunt the chambers of the dead,
   Like flowers around the funeral urn.

Yet shall arise upon my way,
  Affection's buds and blossoms fair;
The same that in my early day
  With heavenly fragrance filled the air.

They live—they breathe; and on my heart
  I wear, still wear those cherished flowers;
And death alone those ties can part,
  First woven in my home's sweet bowers.

O pause, old Time! for though to thee
  I have not brought the tribute due;
And hours, days, years, have fled from me,
  Still to my mortal trust untrue;

Yet, in thy course thou hast not seen,
  Ungenerous wish, or fault unmourned,
And all that ought not to have been
  Upon a sorrowing heart returned.

And ere I bow beneath thy sway,
  Full many a virtue shall be mine;
For I will consecrate each day,
  To bend at duty's hallowed shrine.

Then pause, old Time, ere o'er my flowers,
  Thy fatal sithe is coldly laid;
And leave, O leave, some lingering hours,
  Ere Nature's final debt is paid.

          FROM THE SACRED OFFERING.

THE LILY OF THE VALLEY*.

Fair flower, that, lapt in lowly glade,
Dost hide beneath the greenwood shade,
    Than whom the vernal gale
None fairer wakes on bank or spray,
Our England's lily of the May,
    Our Lily of the vale!

Art thou that " Lily of the field,"
Which, when the Saviour sought to shield
    The heart from blank despair,
He showed to our mistrustful kind
An emblem of the thoughtful mind
    Of God's paternal care?

Not thus, I trow; for brighter shine
To the warm skies of Palestine
    Those children of the East :
There, when mild autumn's early rain
Descends on parched Esdrela's plain,
    And Tabor's oak-girt crest;

* The Editor has taken a liberty (for which the beauty
of the language as well as the poetry must plead her excuse)
of extracting this piece from " *The British Months*," a poem
in twelve parts, by Dr. Mant, Lord Bishop of Down and
Connor, recently published by Mr. Parker, West Strand.

More frequent than the host of night,
Those earth-born stars, as sages write,
   Their brilliant disks unfold;
Fit symbol of imperial state,
Their sceptre-seeming forms elate,
   And crowns of burnished gold.

But not the less, sweet spring-tide's flower,
Dost thou display the Maker's power,
   His skill and handywork;
Our western valleys' humbler child,
Where, in green nook of woodland wild,
   Thy modest blossoms lurk.

What though nor care nor art be thine,
The loom to ply, the thread to twine,
   Yet, born to bloom and fade,
Thee too a lovelier robe arrays,
Than, e'en in Israel's brightest days,
   Her wealthiest king arrayed.

Of thy twin leaves the embowered screen,
Which wraps thee in thy shroud of green;
   Thy Eden-breathing smell;
Thy arched and purple-vested stem,
Whence pendent many a pearly gem,
   Displays a milk-white bell.

Instinct with life thy fibrous root,
Which sends from earth the ascending shoot,
   As rising from the dead,

s

And fills thy veins with verdant juice,
Charged thy fair blossoms to produce,
   And berries scarlet red.

The triple cell, the twofold seed,
A ceaseless treasure-house decreed,
   Whence aye thy race may grow,
As from creation they have grown,
While Spring shall weave her flowery crown,
   Or vernal breezes blow.

Who forms thee thus, with unseen hand?
Who at creation gave command,
   And willed thee thus to be;
And keeps thee still in being, through
Age after age revolving?   Who
   But the great God is he?

Omnipotent to work his will;
Wise, who contrives each part to fill
   The post to each assigned;
Still provident, with sleepless care,
To keep, to make thee sweet and fair
   For man's enjoyment—kind!

" There is no God," the senseless say :—
" O God! why cast'st thou us away, ?"
   Of feeble faith and frail,
The mourner breathes his anxious thought :—
By thee a better lesson taught,
   Sweet lily of the vale!

Yes, He who made and fosters thee,
In reason's eye perforce must be
        Of majesty divine.
Nor deems she, that his guardian care
Will He in man's support forbear,
        Who thus provides for thee.

THE SNOW-DROP.

LONE flower, hemmed in with snows as white as they,
But hardier far, once more I see thee bend
Thy forehead, as if fearful to offend,
Like an unbidden guest.   Though day by day,
Storms, sallying from the mountain-tops, waylay
The rising sun, and on the plains descend ;
Yet art thou welcome, welcome as a friend
Whose zeal outruns his promise.   Blue-eyed May
Shall soon behold this border thickly set
With bright jonquils, their odours lavishing
On the soft west wind and his frolic peers ;
Nor will I then thy modest grace forget,
Chaste snowdrop, vent'rous harbinger of spring,
And pensive monitor of fleeting years !

                                    WORDSWORTH.
        s 2

TO A PRIMROSE,

PRESENTED TO A FRIEND, JANUARY, 1829.

SWEET herald of the ever-gentle Spring,
How gently waved o'er thee the Winter's wing!
Around thee blew the warm Favonian gale,
Devonia nursed thee in her loveliest vale;
Beneath she rolled the Plym's pellucid stream,
And Heaven diffused around its quickening beam.
But, ah! the sun, the shower, the zephyr bland,
Made thee but fair to tempt the spoiler's hand.
I cannot bear thee to thy bank again,
And bathe thy breast in soft refreshing rain,
Nor bid the gentle zephyr round thee play,
Nor 'raptured eye thee basking in the ray;
But snapped untimely from thy velvet stem,
Be thou my daily care, my " bonnie gem,"
And when thus severed from thy native glade,
The radiance of thy cinque-rayed star shall fade,
And pale decay come creeping o'er thy bloom,
A sigh, dear flower, shall mourn thy early doom.

N. T. CARRINGTON.

APRIL FLOWERS.

Nor, April, fail with scent and hue,
To grace thee lowlier blossoms new.
Not only that, where weak and scant
Peep'd forth the early primrose plant,
Now shine profuse unnumbered eyes,
Like stars that stud the wint'ry skies;
But that its sister cowslip's nigh,
With no unfriendly rivalry
Of form and tint, and fragrant smells,
O'er the green fields their yellow bells
Unfold, bedropt with tawny red,
And meekly bend the drooping head.
Not only that the fringed edge
Of heath, or bank, or pathway hedge,
Glows with the furze's golden bloom;
But mingling now, the verdant broom,
With flowers of rival lustre deck'd,
Uplifts its shapelier form erect.
    And there upon the sod below,
Ground-ivy's purple blossoms show,
Like helmet of crusader knight,
Its anthers' crosslike forms of white;
And lesser periwinkle's bloom,
Like carpet of Damascus' loom,

Pranks with bright blue the tissue wove,
Of verdant foliage : and above,
With milk-white flowers, whence soon shall swell,
Rich fruitage, to the taste and smell
Pleasant alike, the strawberry weaves
Its coronets of three-fold leaves,
In mazes through the sloping wood.
Nor wants there, in her dreamy mood,
What fancy's sportiveness may think
A cup, whence midnight elves might drink
Delicious drops of nectar'd dew,
While they their fairy sports pursue,
And roundelays by fount or rill ;
The streaked and chequered daffodil.

Nor wants there many a flower beside,
On holt, and hill, and meadow pied ;
With pale green bloom the upright box,
And woodland crowfoot's golden locks ;
And yellow cinquefoil's hairy trail ;
And saxifrage with petals pale ;
And purple bilberry's globelike head ;
And cranberry's bells of rosy red ;
And creeping growwell blue and bright ;
And cranesbill's streaks of red and white,
Or purple, with soft leaves of down ;
And golden tulip's turban'd crown,
Sweet-scented on its bending stem ;
And bright-eyed star of Bethlehem.
With those, the firstlings of their kind,
Which through the bosky thickets wind

Their tendrils, vetch, or pea, or tare,
At random ; and with many a pair
Of leafits green the brake embower,
And many a pendent-painted flower.

FROM BISHOP MANT'S " BRITISH MONTHS.'

THE DEATH OF THE FLOWERS.

How happily, how happily, the flowers die away ;
Oh, could we but return to earth as easily as they!
Just live a life of sunshine, of innocence, and bloom,
Then drop, without decrepitude or pain, into the tomb.

The gay and glorious creatures! they neither " toil nor
    spin;"
Yet, lo! what goodly raiment they're all apparelled in;
No tears are on their beauty, but dewy gems more
    bright,
Than ever brow of eastern queen endiademed with
    light.

The young rejoicing creatures! their pleasures never
    pall ;
Nor lose in sweet contentment, because so free to all!
The dew, the showers, the sunshine, the balmy, blessed
    air,
Spend nothing of their freshness, though all may freely
    share.

The happy, careless creatures! of time they take no
   heed;
Nor weary of his creeping, nor tremble at his speed;
Nor sigh with sick impatience, and wish the light away;
Nor when 'tis gone cry dolefully, " would God that it
   were day!"

And when their lives are over, they drop away to rest,
Unconscious of the penal doom, on holy Nature's breast;
No pain have they in dying, no shrinking from decay:
Oh! could we but return to earth as easily as they!

CAROLINE BOWLES.

THE END.

Bradbury and Evans, Printers, Whitefriars.

A SELECT

LIST OF BOOKS

RE-PUBLISHED BY

HENRY WASHBOURNE, SALISBURY SQUARE.

———

CLARKE'S INTRODUCTION TO HERALDRY.

THE TWELFTH EDITION, revised and improved by new Engravings, of the ENGLISH and SCOTCH REGALIA, ORDERS OF KNIGHTHOOD, &c. &c., illustrated by Historical Notices. Also, a LIST OF FOREIGN ORDERS, and their abbreviations; a DICTIONARY OF 1200 MOTTOES, with the *English Translations* and *Bearers' Names* alphabetically arranged; the ORIGIN AND USE OF ARMS; RULES FOR BLAZONING AND MARSHALLING COAT ARMOURS; a DICTIONARY OF HERALDRY, with its Terms, in English, French, and Latin; DEGREES OF THE NOBILITY AND GENTRY; TABLES OF PRECEDENCY, &c.; embellished with Forty-eight Engravings, illustrative of upwards of 1,000 Examples, including the Arms of above 500 Families. Royal 18mo. Price 20s. with Plates correctly coloured; 9s. plain Plates; and 12s. on paper prepared for Learners to colour.

ELVEN'S HERALDRY OF CRESTS.

A new edition, greatly enlarged and improved,

Comprising the Crests of every Peer and Baronet of Great Britain, and nearly every Family, with a correct List of the Nobility, their Family Names, and copious Indexes of all the Bearers. The whole accompanied by a Dictionary of Terms, and Remarks Historical and Explanatory. Royal 18mo. Bound, 10s., or on prepared paper for colouring, 13s.

A BIBLIOGRAPHICAL, ANTIQUARIAN, AND PICTURESQUE TOUR IN FRANCE AND GERMANY,

By the Rev. THOMAS FROGNALL DIBDIN, D.D. illustrated with Engravings, Fac-similes, &c. 3 vols. post 8vo. In whole cloth and lettered, *published at 2l. 15s., now sold at a very reduced price.*

AN INTRODUCTION TO THE STUDY OF ENGLISH BOTANY,

with a Glossary of Terms; illustrated by Thirty-seven Plates. By GEORGE BANKS, F.L.S. Second Edition, 8vo. Coloured, price 18s., or with plain Plates, price 9s. in cloth.

COLONEL LEITH HAY'S NARRATIVE OF THE PENINSULAR WAR.

Second edition. Twenty-two Engravings. 2 vols. small 8vo. Price 10s. 6d.; originally published at 1l. 1s.

" We are well pleased to see this cheap re-issue of a work which, at its first publication, we commended as a pleasant, honest narrative."—*Athenæum.*

SELECT BIOGRAPHY.

A Collection of Lives of Eminent Persons who have been an honour to their country. 25 finely-engraved Portraits. 12 vols. 18mo. In cloth bds., or 24 parts, sewed. Published at 3l., and now sold at a reduced price. Comprising some of the most Eminent Divines and Philanthropists, States-men and Warriors, Poets and Dramatists, Travellers and Voyagers, Painters and Historians.

TALES OF A PHYSICIAN.

By HARRISON. 2 vols. post 8vo. Price 10s. 6d.

THE ETONIAN.

3 vols. post 8vo. Price 18s.

HERBERT'S COUNTRY PARSON,

his Character, and Rules of Holy Life, &c. Royal 32mo. Price 2s. 6d. cloth; roan embossed, 4s.; or in purple morocco, gilt edges, 5s.

HERBERT'S SACRED POEMS, &c.

Royal 32mo. Price 3s. cloth; roan embossed, 4s. 6d.; morocco, 5s. 6d.

HERBERT'S COUNTRY PARSON, AND SACRED POEMS;

with his LIFE, from IZAAK WALTON. In one volume royal 32mo. Price 5s. cloth; roan embossed, 6s. 6d.; morocco, 7s. 6d.

EASY INTRODUCTION TO SHORT-HAND.

For Schools and Private Tuition. Royal 18mo. Price 1s. 6d.

THE HORSE,

in all its Varieties and Uses. By JOHN LAWRENCE. Second Edition, with a Portrait, royal 12mo. Price 6s. cloth and lettered.

PLAIN ADVICE TO LANDLORDS AND TE-NANTS, LODGING-HOUSE KEEPERS AND LODGERS;

with a Summary of the Law of Distress, the Powers vested in Tax-collectors, Parochial Authorities, &c. A New Edition. Price 1s. 6d.

" It contains a good deal of practical information in a concise form, unobscured by legal technicalities. There is an excellent Summary of the Law of Distress."—*Times.*

A FAMILIAR SUMMARY OF THE LAW OF MASTER AND SERVANT, APPRENTICES,

&c. 18mo. Price 1s. 6d.

MELMOTH'S GREAT IMPORTANCE OF A RELIGIOUS LIFE, with Morning and Evening Prayers. Royal 32mo. fine paper, 1s. sewed; 1s. 6d. in extra cloth and lettered; 2s. silk or elegantly bound in morocco, 5s.

TALBOT'S REFLECTIONS for Every Day of the Week; with Thoughts on various Subjects, Poems, &c. Royal 32mo., with vignette, &c. Price 1s.; silk 2s.; or bound with MELMOTH, in one Vol. 3s. silk; morocco, 6s.

FENELON'S PIOUS THOUGHTS concerning the Knowledge and Love of God, and other Holy Exercises; with an engraved portrait and title. 32mo. Price 1s. sewed; in roan or in a case with gilt edges, 1s. 6d.; morocco, 4s.; or silk, elegant, 2s.

FENELON'S PIOUS REFLECTIONS for Every Day of the Month, with a fine portrait, and Life of the Author. 32mo. At the same prices.

FENELON'S THOUGHTS AND REFLECTIONS, in one volume. 32mo. Price 2s. boards; silk, 3s.; or in morocco. 5s.

JOHNSON'S (Dr.) PRAYERS, &c. 32mo. boards, 9d.; or in silk, 2s.; morocco, 4s.; black sheep, 2s.

THE NEW WEEK'S PREPARATION, for a worthy receiving of the LORD'S SUPPER; consisting of MEDITATIONS AND PRAYERS, Forms of Examination. A COMPANION TO THE ALTAR, &c. Two parts, royal 32mo. Black sheep, 3s.; elegantly embossed, 4s. 6d.; morocco, 7s. Each part separate, black sheep, 2s.; elegantly embossed, 3s.; morocco, 5s. 6d.

WILBERFORCE'S PRACTICAL VIEW OF CHRISTIANITY, with an interesting Memoir of his Life. 18mo., cloth and lettered. Price 3s.

BUTLER'S ANALOGY OF RELIGION. The new STUDENT'S EDITION, 18mo. cloth, 3s. 6d.

BUTLER'S ANALOGY, &c. with his THREE SERMONS on HUMAN NATURE. 18mo. cloth, 4s. 6d. Also the Three Sermons separate, 1s. 6d.

MATTHEW HENRY'S COMMUNICANT'S COMPANION—for the right receiving of the LORD'S SUPPER. A new edition, small 8vo. Price 3s. 6d.

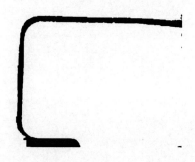

Lightning Source UK Ltd.
Milton Keynes UK
UKOW021946120312

188825UK00008B/106/P